# DREAMER

# TO

# ENTREPRENEUR

## XI Steps to Become a Successful Startup Entrepreneur



DR. SURESH JAIN

Qurate
quratebooks.com

DREAMER TO ENTREPRENEUR
XI Steps to Become a Successful Startup Entrepreneur
Dr. Suresh Jain

Published by Qurate Books Pvt. Ltd.



Published in 2023



**ISBN:** 978-81-19263-38-7

qurate
qURatebooks.com

**Qurate Books Pvt. Ltd.**
Goa 403523, India
www.quratebooks.com
Tel: 1800-210-6527, Email: info@quratebooks.com

**P. NARAHARI** I.A.S.
Secretary Cum Commissioner,
MSME

**Directorate of Industries, M.P.**
(Deptt. of Micro, Small & Medium Enterprises)

D.O. No. PS/MSME/297
Bhopal, Dated 16-06-2023

## Words of Wisdom

Introducing "Dreamer to Entrepreneurs" written by Dr. Suresh Jain, a practical guide tailored for startup entrepreneurs. With 32 thoughtfully structured chapters, the book offers invaluable strategies for entrepreneurial success. Dr. Jain's expertise in finance equips him to address the specific needs of startup entrepreneurs, covering topics from strategic planning to financial management. Fundraising, crisis management, and risk assessment are also explored. The book emphasizes the significance of mindset, motivation, and resilience, empowering readers to overcome challenges. "Dreamer to Entrepreneur" provides a blueprint for success, drawing on Dr. Suresh Jain's wealth of knowledge and practical insights. Whether staring a business or seeking expansion, this guide offers essential tools and strategies. It is recommended for entrepreneurs in need of inspiration and expertise, Prepare for a remarkable journey of self-discovery and achievement of goal to become a successful startup entrepreneur.

My best wishes to all aspiring and existing entrepreneurs and congratulations to the author for such a wonderful book to guide the entrepreneurs.

P Narahari IAS

# FOREWORD - 1

Starting your own business can be an exciting and well-rewarding experience. It makes one self-reliant while providing others with job opportunities. The right skills and attitude are must for an entrepreneur to thrive in this changing economy.

Entrepreneurs are people that are blessed with the capacity to dream and take the risks that make the dream come true. Making a business profitable is not easy - it requires planning, proper execution and understanding of the needs of people around you. This book does exactly that - provides you with a step-by-step guide on how to make the most of your time and become successful entrepreneurs. The Author Dr Suresh Jain with his vast experience in banking, credit, and entrepreneurship development, has shared his valuable knowledge and experience on entrepreneurship in this book. His easy-to-understand style of writing will engage an aspirant entrepreneur in becoming a successful one. I congratulate Dr. Suresh Jain for this inspiring book that will enlighten the reader on all business-related topics. I hope the reader gets motivated to pursue the field of entrepreneurship with enhanced clarity and hope for a brighter future.

**Amit Goel**
**[A Promising Entrepreneur]**
**Founder and Managing Director - Prodigee Finance Limited**
**Founder – Prodigee Private Limited**
**Founder – Credgenix Private Limited**

**Date – 23rd May 2023**

**Place- Bhopal [M.P.] India 462011**

**Dr. B.N. Singh**
*Ph.d (Austria) FNAVS*
*Director Management*

Mob. : (O) 0755-2740395
(R) 0755-2759667
Website : www.rkdf.ac.in
Email : drbnsingh@rkdf.ac.in

# RKDF UNIVERSITY

(ESTABLISHED UNDER GOVT. OF M.P. AND APPROVED UNDER UGC 2(F) 1956)

No. 1077 /RKDF/2023 Dated : 29/05/2023

## Foreword

When you think about yourself as a successful entrepreneur, what types of image or feelings you experienced? Do you find yourself dreaming about creating the next great solution to society's problem? May be you can imagine yourself creating something that equally balance art, function and ingenuity. I am happy to explore that this book is designed to help you to develop your entrepreneurial vision. Vision is an important part of everyone's future, and this is especially true for entrepreneurs. Establishing your vision is the first of several steps toward making your venture a reality.

This book is the perfect place to start if you are unable to think and feel yourself as an entrepreneur. May be you have only worked ever for other peoples or still thinking out what your career should look like. This book will really help you to understand actual concept of entrepreneur and how it helps you to be a great leader. Different chapters of this book cover strategic business plan preparation, basic of balance sheet, preparation of project report, project appraisal, time management, crisis management and customer relationship management etc.

In this Dr. Suresh Jain highlighted most significant issues related to entrepreneur **"Dreamer to Entrepreneur"**

I hearty congratulate Dr. Suresh Jain for his valuable book that will enlighten everyone on all topic related to business title or topic. This book helps reader to get motivated themselves in order to looking forward a bright future

(Dr. B. N. Singh)
Director Management
RKDF University, Bhopal

# PROLOGUE

Dear Reader,

I am delighted to introduce "Dreamer to Entrepreneur," an insightful and practical guide written by Dr. Suresh Jain, a veteran banker, and esteemed financial consultant. This book has been meticulously crafted to assist MSME entrepreneurs in realizing their dreams and overcoming the challenges they face in setting up, running, and expanding their businesses.

Within its 32 thoughtfully structured chapters, "Dreamer to Entrepreneur" takes you on a transformative journey, providing invaluable guidance and strategies to navigate the path towards entrepreneurial success. Dr. Suresh's vast experience and expertise in the field of finance have uniquely positioned him to address the specific needs of startup entrepreneurs, offering them a comprehensive roadmap towards achieving their goals.

The book encompasses a wide range of essential topics crucial for entrepreneurial success. From strategic planning and leadership to product development and financial management, Dr. Suresh leaves no stone unturned. Chapters dedicated to fundraising, time and crisis management, project appraisal, and risk management equip readers with the necessary tools to overcome obstacles and make informed decisions.

Moreover, "Dreamer to Entrepreneur" delves into the often-overlooked aspect of entrepreneur psychology, highlighting the significance of mindset, motivation, and resilience in the face of challenges. Dr. Suresh's deep understanding of the human psyche, combined with his practical advice, empowers readers to develop the mental fortitude required for their entrepreneurial journey.

I am confident that "Dreamer to Entrepreneur" will prove to be an invaluable companion for aspiring and struggling entrepreneurs alike. It offers a blueprint for success, underpinned by Dr. Suresh's wealth of knowledge and practical insights. Whether you are just starting out or seeking guidance to expand your existing business, this book will provide you with the essential tools and strategies to transform your dreams into reality.

I wholeheartedly recommend "Dreamer to Entrepreneur" to all entrepreneurs seeking inspiration, guidance, and expertise. Prepare to embark on a remarkable journey of self-discovery and entrepreneurial achievement.

Wishing you every success on your path to entrepreneurship!

Sincerely,

**[Ajay Vyas]**

Financial Consultant, Digital Banking Strategist Innovator

Former Executive Director UCO Bank

# INDEX

CHAPTER 1

# Introduction

The word 'entrepreneur' is derived from the french word 'entreprende'. It means to' undertake'. Richard Cantilon who is a french Banker used the term *entrepreneur in 18th century first time in economic activities* to mean a person who bears uncertainty and risk.

Thus, the concept of entrepreneur and entrepreneurship is age old concept and many authors have defined it in their own ways. I quote hereunder definitions of some eminent authorities.

Peter F Drucker one of the most widely known authors and influential thinkers on Management states that an entrepreneur is the one who always searches for changes, responds to it and exploits it as an opportunity. He further states that innovation is the specific tool of an entrepreneur, the means by which he exploits change as an opportunity for a different business or services.

## Schumpeter:

A well-known author has defined entrepreneur as an individual who carries out new combines of means of production by which there occurs disequilibrium."

According to him "The entrepreneur, in an advanced economy is an individual who introduces something new in the economy - a method of production not yet tested by experience in the branch of manufacturing, a product with which consumers are not yet familiar, a new source of raw material or of new markets and the like".

He stated that the "entrepreneur is an individual who exploits market opportunity through technical and/or organization innovation. Thus, the entrepreneur is basically an innovator and innovator are one who introduces new combinations.

After looking to the definition of the entrepreneur its important here to look into the definition of eminent authors on entrepreneurship.

1. "Entrepreneurship means the function of seeing investment and production opportunity, organizing an enterprise to undertake a new production process, raising capital, hiring labour, arranging for supply of raw materials and selecting top managers for day-to-day operations of the enterprise." - Higgins
2. "Entrepreneurship is essentially a creative activity, or it is an innovation function. The process of innovation may be in the form of -
   (a) Introduction of a new product.
   (b) Use of a new method of production.
   (c) Opening of a new market.
   (d) The conquest of new source of supplying raw material.
   (e) A new form of organization." - Joseph A. Schumpeter
3. "Entrepreneurship is defined as a systematic innovation, which consists in the purposeful and organized search for changes, and it is the systematic analysis of the opportunities. Such changes might offer economic and social innovation." **Peter F. Drucker.**
4. "Entrepreneurship is the purposeful activity of an individual or a group of associated individuals, undertaken to initiate, maintain or organize a profit-oriented business unit for the production or distribution of economic goods and services". - A. H. Cole

5. "Entrepreneurship is the investing and risking of time, money and effort to start a business and make it successful." - Musscleman and Jackson

6. "Entrepreneurship involves a wide range of areas on which a series of decisions are required which can be grouped into three categories -

   (a) perception of an opportunity.

   (b) organizing an industrial unit.

   (c) running the industrial unit as a profitable, going, and growing concern." - Higgins

In the above backdrop, we may define in a simple way that the entrepreneur is an individual who creates an innovative idea to develop a new product, process, or service and thereby establish a new business enterprise or scale up an existing business enterprise, take calculative financial risk and find out how to mitigate such risk and gain the profit. In other words, an entrepreneur is someone who develops a business model, starts it as his/her new venture operationalizes it, and takes responsibility for its success or failure. Entrepreneurs should have a clear mindset to establish the enterprises with full knowledge of risk and reward and must have confidence in themselves with a clear vision to establish and scale up their business. The success of such an enterprise shall depend on the quantum of sale of products and services to its target customers and earn the profit. A successful entrepreneur also keeps in mind to solve the problem and deliver value to the customers by introducing new products or services and expanding its market to make the product and services available within the reach of maximum customers. Being an entrepreneur means carving your own path with courage, confidence, and a positive mindset. An entrepreneur should also build a team of competent experts and employees who are positive, motivated, and committed to making a difference and creating value for the enterprise.

The process of setting up of business enterprise by the entrepreneur bearing the risk and enjoying the reward is termed entrepreneurship.

Entrepreneurship is a creative approach undertaken by an entrepreneur to establish a new business enterprise or scale up an existing business enterprise with an innovative product or process or service. Innovation and risk are integral parts of entrepreneurship. Each enterprise will be successful and have the potential to grow many folds if the product and process are well tested and good demand is created by the promoter with proper strategies and marketing.

Entrepreneurs and entrepreneurship come in many businesses structure like trading, industries, online business, E-Commerce platform, self-employment activities, consultancy, etc. The enterprise can be constituted as a proprietorship firm, partnership firm, limited liability partnership, private limited and public limited companies, etc. A newly started enterprise with innovative products or processes or services falls into the category of a start-up.

Each aspect of entrepreneur and entrepreneurship shall be discussed in the following chapters to ensure the success of all entrepreneurs.

●●●

CHAPTER 2

# Characteristics and Qualities of Entrepreneur

Entrepreneurship is a great opportunity, provided the entrepreneurs possess the entrepreneurial mindset, clear vision, mission, and spirit to overcome the hurdles that may come in the way of their entrepreneurial journey.

Many people wish to become entrepreneurs by starting a new venture but have yet to learn about starting a profitable business. Moreover, they believe that starting a new business enterprise carries a risk or requires a very high educational background, like a degree in business management or technical skill, previous business experience, etc. Their above apprehensions are invalid, looking to facts that entrepreneurs come from every section of society. Aspiring entrepreneurs must acquire some knowledge, skill, and risk assessment and mitigation process concerning the business activity they want to establish. The knowledge and skill boost their confidence to achieve their dream.

After that, aspiring Entrepreneurs can start planning and executing their new venture with a positive mindset and self-confidence to become successful start-up entrepreneurs.

We discuss hereunder in detail the characteristics and qualities of entrepreneurs.

1. **Mind Set** - The entrepreneurial mindset combines education, training, experience, skills, beliefs, and thought processes. A positive mindset is necessary to

start a new venture or start-up. People should have strong willpower to become a successful entrepreneur. They should enjoy the proud moments of being their own boss instead of working for someone else as their employees. When entrepreneurs are strongly motivated, their entrepreneurial journey becomes unstoppable. They can also feel the pleasure of being a job provider, not a job seeker. It is worth noting that success comes 80 percent from a mindset and 20 percent from skill; therefore, a growth-oriented mindset evolves abilities to do what one decides. Building skill from what you know gives you simple success, but implementing a promising business idea with a passion and a strong mindset will ensure success, and you will reach the top of the ladder.

2. **Goal Oriented, Self-Confident, and Ambitious** – The entrepreneur should be goal oriented and committed to taking action to achieve the goal. Goal setting is the first step towards the success of the entrepreneurship journey. Entrepreneurs who do not have the attribute to set a goal will not know where they want to go. They should be self-confident, ambitious and believe in their capabilities that they will do it and achieve their goal.

3. **Focused Approach** – Entrepreneurs should focus on achieving their goal within the prefixed timeline. If entrepreneurs continue to divert their attention to so many things at a time, they cannot attend to their primary tasks with due attention and achieve their goals. It's important to mention here that many times it's easy to start an enterprise; still, it requires a certain gestation period to achieve the desired progress, and hence a long-term focus approach is necessary for the enterprise's success. High performers are known to have a pinpoint focus on their immediate task and give their all without worrying about what has happened in the past or what may come up in future.

4. **Action Oriented** – Entrepreneurs should act fast within a short time to achieve their goals. The word like will do it tomorrow, or I will try will not take them anywhere. The action should always be well-defined, and consistent, with a stipulated timeline to reach the target. It's also essential to have an alternate course of action if some hurdles are expected in the initial action plan so that the entrepreneur journey indeed achieves success.

5. **Managerial And Technical Knowledge, Skill, and Team Building** – Entrepreneurs should possess the required Managerial and technical Knowledge and skill relating to their enterprise and continuously improve to become successful entrepreneurs. Those who stay at the top of their position take a keen interest in learning what they lack, not only from formal education but also from observations of what is happening around them and from what life teaches. Their learning habit makes them, as well as their work, better and better every day. The entrepreneurs should also engage a mentor for required guidance and hire subject experts, thereby building a team of competent employees and inculcating team spirit in them; so that, everyone works to create value for the company.

6. **Curiosity And Consistency** - Curiosity keeps entrepreneurs aware of the kind of products and services in high demand, where the market is, and the target group of customers for the sale of such products or services. Entrepreneurs must maintain consistency in their efforts to search for such products and services, which gives them good opportunities to learn and discover new products or services.

7. **Creativity** – Creativity is an important quality of an entrepreneur. Creative entrepreneurs have a better imagination to design products and services and improve them as per the need of their customers.

8. **Adaptability** – Entrepreneurs should be adaptable and remain flexible to the extent possible in changed business scenarios to solve the challenges that come before them during the business cycle and ensure that their business keeps growing as per their business plan.

9. **Decision-Making Capability** – Successful entrepreneurs make quick decisions in every aspect of their business, irrespective of prevailing circumstances. They know that the delay in the decision may turn a simple and routine matter into a complicated issue and may lead to loss to their enterprise.

10. **Innovative Attitude** – A successful entrepreneur should have an innovative attitude and further cultivate it and keep on developing and improving the product, process, and services as per customer's needs.

11. **Risk Analysis and Its Mitigation and Risk Bearing Capacity** - Entrepreneurship carries risk and reward both. A successful entrepreneur analyses the risk and finds out the ways to mitigate it or minimize it. Despite the best efforts many times the risk cannot be fully insulated, under such situation the entrepreneur should absorb the failure and learn from it so that in future such risk can be better insulated in advance.

12. **Fear of Failure** - An entrepreneurs should have a positive mindset and handle unpleasant situations like failure of their business despite of appropriate risk insulation, as a part of the game. They should not carry with them any fear of failure, rather learn the lesson from mistakes and shortcomings, and take appropriate corrective steps treating such failure as a first step of success. Remember everyone deals with the setbacks even those who are today at the top, because they have not given up and taken failure as a first step towards success. SachinTendulkar an Indian cricketer reached to the top in cricket world

because of his persistent efforts and strong will power, though he faced many challenges as a cricket player.

13. **Communication, Leadership and Team Building** - The successful entrepreneurs should possess good communication skills and have leadership qualities. They should build their team of well qualified competent people for the success of their enterprises. Everyone in the enterprise should work as a team to take the enterprise to the new height. Concerning to leadership, it's important that the entrepreneurs should be the thought leaders by establishing their authority as an expert in a specific area of their working, building a trust among employees and customers and providing innovative solutions to industry challenges and innovative products, process, and services to their enterprises. Thought leadership qualities in the entrepreneurs will make their enterprises outstanding among the other enterprises, and they become the source of inspiration to others in addition to winning performance of their enterprises.

14. **Understand Basic Banking, Finance and Accounts** - It's important for the entrepreneurs to understand basic banking, finance, and accounts to run their enterprises successfully. Successful entrepreneurs make quick decisions in every aspect of their business, irrespective of prevailing circumstances. They know that the delay in the decision may turn a simple and routine matter into a complicated issue and may lead to loss to their enterprise. Successful entrepreneurs make quick decisions in every aspect of their business, irrespective of prevailing circumstances. They know that the delay in the decision may turn a simple and routine matter into a complicated issue and may lead to loss to their enterprise.

15. **Resiliency-** The entrepreneurs should stand with pressure, failure and challenges that comes in their way

of entrepreneurial journey. At the same time, they should learn the lessons from above unpleasant experiences and take required precautionary action to overcome them to continue their entrepreneurship journey unaffected.

To sum up, entrepreneurs should possess or develop the above characteristics and qualities essential for the success of the entrepreneurship journey.

●●●

CHAPTER 3

# Mindset and Attitude Matters most for an Entrepreneur

An entrepreneur is a person who sets up his own enterprise taking calculative risk for perceived rewards. He initiates the idea, formulates a plan, organizes resources and puts the plan into action to achieve his goal. Entrepreneurs have specific characteristics, qualities, and special strengths, which they draw upon their adventure into entrepreneurship and play different roles at different stages of entrepreneurship. An entrepreneur must possess a positive and action-oriented mindset which is explained below.

1. **Dream It; Take Action to Achieve It:**

   Entrepreneurs need to have clear vision and mission and a strong winning mindset to make their dreams come true. They build strategic business planning, decide their goal, and take action to achieve it with excellence. They further move on to spot the growth opportunities and go head to includes the same in for their expansion or diversification business plan. On the other hand, the people who do not have entrepreneurial mindset are found reluctant to take action to make their dream a reality.

2. **Self-Commitment:**

   Entrepreneurs should know the art of selective discipline, their vision and mission, which will decide their line of action to achieve their goal for which they should remain committed always. Difficulties and problems, or challenges whatever comes in their way can be resolved by them with their best of abilities and flexibility in their action plan. They work not only hard but also smartly until successful completion of their mission.

3. **Treat Risk as a Part of Game:**

   Entrepreneurs know that risk is part of any business enterprises. They smartly analyse the risk and find out the ways to mitigate the risk to the extent possible. However, in situations where mitigation of risk is not possible in toto, they choose the risk where there are good chance to win exist, but they don't give up easily. They take onus of their decisions in their entrepreneurial journey.

4. **Keen Observer and In-Cash Opportunity:**

   Entrepreneurs keep their eyes and year open, observe carefully what is trailing and what are the emerging opportunities available and accordingly their innovative mind start to plan carefully, to convert their observations into business opportunities.

5. **Only Business Matters:**

   Entrepreneurs are fully dedicated to their business commitments. Their personal likes and dislikes do not matter for them in their business verticals. They appoint mentors or professionals rather than friends and relatives when any guidance and support is required. They have a practical and realistic approach to business matters without giving any importance to the emotional aspect.

6. **Customers Centric:**

   Entrepreneurs take the feedback of customer seriously with sportsman spirit whether the same are favourable or unfavourable. In fact, they feel good about favourable customers reaction but feel more excited and energetic with unfavourable reactions because it gives them a chance to improve their product and services which will ultimately bring success to their venture.

7. **Optimistic:**

   Entrepreneurs have an optimistic mindset. They always remain sure of their success without getting affected by any negativity which may come across during their entrepreneurial journey.

8. **Influencer:**

   An entrepreneur should act as an influencer to make the people buy the products and services made available to people by his enterprise. This will increase the sales, which is the backbone of success of any enterprise.

9. **Long Term Player:**

   An entrepreneurs should think of remaining in his business for the long term once they have decided to set up the same. They should have a long-term goal to scale up their business activities to many folds in years to come.

**The above qualities at mindset level will lead to sure success to the entrepreneurs to achieve their goals.**

●●●

CHAPTER 4

# XI Steps to Become a Successful Startup Entrepreneur

The following XI steps are important for making proper strategies and planning to become a successful startup entrepreneur.

**STEP – I.**

The first step for the entrepreneurs is to conduct a market survey or a market study to understand the need of the customers to develop the products/processes/services accordingly. Such products, processes, and services will have a robust market and ready buyers, and it will be easy to develop a broader market of such products/processes and services in the near future.

**STEP – II.**

In the second step, the entrepreneurs should identify opportunities for innovative products/processes/services based on a market survey or market study/own assessment/idea generation/fusion of ideas/and ease of doing business. The customer's needs, choices, tastes, preferences, and market trends for the product have prime importance in the identification of opportunities.

**STEP – III**

The third step is to conceptualize and develop a prototype of innovative products, processes, or services by crystallizing the selection and validation of opportunity by ascertaining the demand for the products or processes, or services in the market and by running a trial run among some customers and obtaining the feedback of such customers. If the market report and feedback of the customers are positive, the entrepreneurs may move ahead with the final selection of innovative products/processes/services. Selection of products/processes/services that resolve some problem or make the life of the customers easy or cost-effective with better quality compared to similar products are easy to position at a high level in the market.

The above stage is called the seed stage in startup journey.

### STEP - IV.

In the fourth step, the entrepreneurs should appoint a mentor [if required] and get their guidance to start the entrepreneurial journey. The mentor will guide at every stage of the implementation of a project. The valuable advice of a mentor will increase the project's success rate many folds. Startup entrepreneurs should also approach incubation centres established in many reputed institutions/ universities with their concept and prototype for necessary guidance from subject experts and financial support to develop the product as per their concept and prototype.

### STEP - V.

In the fifth step, entrepreneurs must take action on many things, like preparing a business model based on innovative products/processes/ services. This model should explain the type of business like trading, manufacturing, or services, organize the product/process or services prototype, prepare the road map to manufacture the products, or develop the processes and services with technical specifications. The entrepreneurs should also prepare the estimation of sales and profit with future outlook, target customers, and plan to capture the market for the sale of the products/processes/services. The model should also cover the estimated funds required and sources of funds to meet the requirement to start and run the business enterprises.

## STEP – VI.

The sixth step is to appoint the subject experts and team members and delegate the work and powers to make decisions in the interest of the enterprises. For the project's success, the team members from top to bottom shall need to align to achieve the goal of the enterprise in respect of every vertical, including customer satisfaction.

## STEP – VII.

In the seventh step, the entrepreneurs should constitute the business firm, such as a proprietorship firm, partnership firm, Pvt Ltd company, or a company limited by shares or limited liability partnership [LLP], and obtain all necessary registration, licenses, approvals as applicable from the competent authorities and applicable laws.

## STEP – VIII.

The eighth step is for the preparation of the business plan with an implementation schedule and making a project report with projections of financials for the next 5 years to arrive at the conclusion that the project is technically feasible and financially viable. Also crystallize future outlook to scale up the business.

## STEP – IX.

The ninth step is to arrange the funds from various sources, including grants, aids, subsidies, [if available] private equity, venture capital funds, and Bank finance for the project. To complete the process of fund arrangement in the shortest possible time, the entrepreneurs may hire experts as the sanction process require systemically drafting of the proposal and many supporting documents and information about the project and promoters. Establish the production unit following the details mentioned in the project report and complete the project as per the implementation schedule. As envisaged in the project report, ensuring the unit comes to production on or before the commercial operation date is vital. Entrepreneurs must also ensure that the unit achieves the estimated sale volume and profit.

### STEP - X.

In the tenth step, the entrepreneurs should create brand, logo, website and Marketing strategies. Brand creation and logo will build the image and acceptability of the products, processes and services in the market. The ultimate progress of the enterprise will come from the sale of the products/processes and services. Likewise creating own website also build the brand value, market reputation and contribute to the marketing of the products/processes and services.

This stage is called the operational stage in startup entrepreneurial journey.

### STEP - XI.

The eleventh step is the scaling-up stage, when the startup enterprise grows many folds and achieves new milestones in production, sales volume, and profit, thereby creating value for the investors and entrepreneurs. To scale up the business, the entrepreneur should explore new markets, go with a deeper penetration in existing markets, modify or change the product design as per the customers' needs, and change the printing and packaging according to customers' liking and business trends. These honest and sincere efforts will undoubtedly result in the scaling-up of the enterprises.

To sum up, all the above steps are self-explanatory. Startup entrepreneurs should start their journey and move step by step to become successful startup entrepreneurs.

●●●

CHAPTER 5

# Entrepreneurship- A Matter of Pride for Entrepreneur

Entrepreneurship is the most exciting opportunity of self-employment. A great feeling of "be your own boss" can be achieved through entrepreneurship only. In employment one works for others, and one works as others want one to do. There is no scope for doing as you wish, doing what you wish, doing how you wish. But in entrepreneurship you work for yourself, achieve a target or a goal set by yourself and reap the satisfaction of having achieved the goal yourself.

Entrepreneurship is not a matter of hereditary. It is 80 percent mind set and 20 percent skill. It is individual potentialities irrespective of any caste, community and class, or economic background. It is not necessary that one should be highly educated or should have vast experience, rather a workable knowledge and skill are sufficient provided he possesses a strong mind set, high ambition, passion and fighting spirit to succeed as an entrepreneur apart from other qualities mentioned in this book. As such, any person having a positive mindset, passion, ambition, fighting spirit and aptitude to do in him/her can become an entrepreneur. A person can get required knowledge and skill from various sources/training institutes and universities if he is determined to become a successful entrepreneur.

Some more material reasons to feel proud of entrepreneurship:

1. It provides an opportunity to get into a process which leads to the realization of an individual's passion for innovation and development. Its well-known facts that entrepreneurship have been the origin of many radical innovations.

2. It is through science and technology inputs that modern technology can be introduced in various sector of economy and thereby a new cost effectiveness and sophistication can be brought in the products and processes as well as in services to be utilized by the people at large.

3. To find suitable employment one must try hard but may or may not get success. On the other end to be an entrepreneur one must believe in himself and if the qualities and competencies are there, he will succeed in becoming an entrepreneur. There may be challenges that come in entrepreneurial journey but can be crossed over with entrepreneur mindset easily. Entrepreneurship is not tough as it is thought by many aspirants.

4. The Government and many universities offer so many facilities like selection of viable products/processes/services, appropriate business model, mentoring, and providing incentives to help new entrepreneurs for their enterprises and startups.

5. An entrepreneur is his/her own boss who creates employment for others and in this way he/she becomes a source of livelihood for so many people, which is a great service to the society of the country.

Entrepreneur develops innovative products and services which becomes growth engine of many economies. The google, face book, e-commerce, smart phone, Artificial Intelligence, are the examples which has impacted every one's life and changed the world to a great extend in last 20 years.

To sum up, entrepreneurship contributes significantly to society at large, and at the same time, it functions as a growth engine for the country's economy, giving a sense of pride to the entrepreneurs.

●●●

CHAPTER 6

# Types of Entrepreneurships

Entrepreneurs have many business opportunities and according to type of business, size of operation, Nature of business, Economic sector, entrepreneurs' personality, entrepreneurship is categorized into different types. We discuss hereunder some common types of entrepreneurships.

1. **Based on Type of Business Activity: -**

   A] **Trading entrepreneurship** – Trading is basically the purchase of products in bulk and sale of the same in wholesale or retail. This also covers trading on the E. Commerce platform or through our own website. Dealership, franchisee, distributorship will fall into this category. This is one of the simplest forms of entrepreneurship and does not require any specific technical knowledge except managerial skill.

   B] **Manufacturing Entrepreneurship** – This type of entrepreneurship involves manufacturing, processing, and packaging of the products. It requires setting up manufacturing/ processing and packaging facilities for manufacturing the products, from raw material.

   C] **Agricultural entrepreneurship** – This type of entrepreneurship is related to agriculture like cultivation, of agricultural produce including horticulture, aromatic and medicinal plants, etc. and preservation and marketing their Agri- produce. This also covers activities allied to agriculture like Dairy, poultry, Sheep and Goat farming, etc. The entrepreneurs undertake above activities are called Agripreneurs and they introduce innovative and modern practices in their agricultural business activities.

2. **Based on Size of Business:**

A] **Small business entrepreneurship** – It covers small size enterprise usually started by one entrepreneur and not having any ready plan to scale up the business or to go for giving franchisee in future. Examples are hair cutting saloon, Spa, laundry, grocery store etc. This kind of business employee local employees or family members and use their own funds to start the business or take small ticket loan from banks or financial institutions.

B] **Scalable startup entrepreneurship** - As the name suggest this type of business or start up are set up with aim of rapid expansion in terms sales turn and profit. Such entrepreneurs are usually visionary and have long term goals to achieve big profit for themselves and to create value for their investor. The startup entrepreneur looks forward to meeting the capital required for expansion from various sources like venture capital, grant in aid, private funding in equity and debt, and credit facilities such as term loan and working capital from banks. Most of such business enterprises are set up with modern technology, work with proper system and procedure based on Information technology so that proper linkage of different verticals of business can be established and having a good team of experts and employees to scale up the business and create the value both for the entrepreneurs and their investors. Many companies are created with a simple business model but now become the big players, like OLA, Uber, Zomato, Face book, Google, Amazon who has changed the world as on date.

C] **Large company entrepreneurship** - These are already well-established companies like Google, Microsoft and they go on expanding their business worldwide. They continue to make innovations and develop new products relating to their main products. Many times, whenever the opportunity comes, they go for acquisition of other companies whose business relates to their key business and gets bigger in size in respect of turnover and profitability.

**3. Based on Clearance Danhof –**

A] **Innovative Entrepreneurship** - In an innovative entrepreneurship, the entrepreneurs introduce innovative products/ process/ services and find out the customers to buy the same. Many times, business is started with simple but innovative business models and thereafter upgraded products/process or services are introduced or new innovative products/process/ services are added for scaling up the Business. Innovative entrepreneurships are usually started as start up and go for scaling up or expansion in terms of sales and profit.

B] **Imitative Entrepreneurship** - In this type of entrepreneurship, the entrepreneur gets an idea of innovative products/process from other entrepreneurs. They adopt techniques and technology innovated by others and make some improvement in the same and make new combination of product/process and services. They also make their own risk assessment and risk insulation strategies.

C] **Fabian entrepreneurship** - In this type, the entrepreneurs are having a very cautious approach and accept the changes in their business model till they become sure that not adopting such changes may result in loss to their enterprises.

D] Drone entrepreneurship- In this type, entrepreneurs do not accept any changes in product formulae or process even at the possibilities of reduction in sales and profit.

**4. Hustler Entrepreneurship** – A hustler in the business world is commonly known as a self-starter. Hence it can be understood that the entrepreneurship journey started as a self-starter by the entrepreneurs with confidence, having a clear goal to succeed is termed as Hustler entrepreneurship. Entrepreneurs are highly motivated, and they identify and in cash the available opportunities fearlessly to establish and grow their business enterprises.

**5. Social Entrepreneurship** - Social entrepreneurs create a business model which benefits society at large and yields profit for the entrepreneur. Social entrepreneurship may be non-profit also. Some social entrepreneurship also covers aspects like creating self-employment, or work for protection of environment or health and sanitation or running educational programs. Providing banking services or non-banking financial companies services in unserved areas or creating microfinance institutions to provide credit facilities to poor section of society also falls within the social entrepreneurship.

•••

CHAPTER 7

# Process of Identification of Innovative Products/ Processes/ Services [PPS]

The road map of process of identification of innovative products/process or services [in short named as PPS] need a systematic approach to reach winning, niche PPS. Anyone who wishes to be a successful entrepreneur can do it if he is creative, visionary, with a goal oriented positive mind set and action taker. The stages for innovation are described as under-.

1] **Curiosity** - Entrepreneur should have a curiosity to observe the world with a business angle. Like what are need of the people or what can make the life of people easy or comfortable or how the heath conditions can be improved by prevention of disease, accurate and quick diagnosis of disease and support to the doctors or specialists to decides the appropriate treatment, or what kind of changes in the existing industries or enterprise can increase the production or can reduced the cost of products or can bring more precision and automation by artificial intelligence, machine learning and robotics.

2] **Creativity** - Once curiosity identifies the area suitable for your passion, the same is to be pursued further by your creativity. Creation of road map for innovation of some PPS in your area of interest, making systemic study of demand and supply position and estimated risk and reward to arrive at most suitable PPS to start with the entrepreneurship journey.

3] **Idea generation** - The curious and creative mind generates the ideas which lead to innovation. The ideas in its totality may not be a new one but it may be a new version of old ideas or fusion of ideas by adopting better methodology. We mention below famous quote of the well-known Indian author Shiv Kheda that.

"Winners don't do different things; they do things differently."

This different way of doing things has become an innovative idea for entrepreneurs for further development of PPS.

Entrepreneurs may develop their confidence that they may derive new ideas from existing ideas to start their entrepreneurial journey. Let's learn from quote of Samuel Langhorne Clemens known by his pen name **Mark Twain**, an American writer, humourist, and entrepreneur who explained the idea generation intricacies as below:

"There is no such thing as a new idea. It is impossible. We simply take a lot of old ideas and put them into a sort of mental kaleidoscope. We give them a turn, and they make new and curious combinations. We keep on turning and making new combinations indefinitely; but they are the same old pieces of coloured glass that have been in use through all the ages."

There are ample examples of idea generation which has made a successful business venture. The wright brothers were always fascinated to work on different mechanical projects and keeping up with the scientific research. They were following up German Otto Lilienthal aviator. When Lilienthal died, they decided to develop design of airplane. They were trying to figure out how to design the wings. They make observation that birds angle their wings for balance and control and emulate the concept called Wing warping. They added a movable rudder and found that it's a successful formula. This observation succeeded them in flying for the first time, in a well-controlled, power driven, heavier than air, airplane.

The new idea many times comes from fusion of many ideas in existence.

Justin Musk an author (she is ex-wife of Elon Musk, CEO of tesla) explained the fusion of ideas as-

"Choose one thing and become a Master of It. Choose a second thing and become a master of that. When you become a master of two worlds (say, engineering and business), you can bring them together in a way that will a) introduce hot ideas to each other, so they can have idea marriage and **make idea babies that no one has seen before,** and b) create a competitive advantage because you can move between worlds, speak both languages, connect the tribes, **mash the elements to spark fresh creative insight** until you wake up with the epiphany that changes your life."

Such ideas or fusion of ideas, by upgradation, induction of AI, machine learning in the existing system has turned companies like Google, face book, ola, uber, Paytm into very big companies and thereby creating their impact on the life of every person and every economy worldwide.

Here we would like to encourage the entrepreneur to make your thought process creative and analytical to generate new ideas from in and around existing ideas or fusion of idea. We do not say here that absolutely new ideas are not generated, of course generated but it involves research and development which some time may require good number of years to validate the ideas into the new product.

Once the ideas are generated and conceptualized, this is called in other words an innovative idea and products/process/services produced and implemented on such ideas are termed as innovative PPS. The journey of idea generation is nothing but an innovation.

The idea generation is not enough and Entrepreneur to move ahead to next stage of identification of opportunities and thereafter selection or validation of opportunity.

What said by Mark Twain is quoted hereunder.

"A man on new idea is crank until the idea succeeds".

In order to convert the idea into a successful business venture, it is essential to go through the process of identification and selection/validation of opportunity.

Identification of opportunities –

The opportunities are ample, and one must identify it based on ideas generated by him. we quote the views of Douglas MacArthur a famous general in American army, on the opportunity as under.

"There is no security on this earth, - only opportunity".

Once the ideas are generated, the entrepreneur need to examine them what are ideas which can be converted into opportunities in the light of business environment and relevant parameters which may be described as under.

1. Experience/ expertise/ knowledge/ skill and competency of entrepreneur.
2. Entrepreneur own preference for the business activity/ type of products/processes/services.
3. Regulatory norms for the products/processes/services and related industry.
4. Market conditions like demand and supply position.
5. Technological support in the production and distribution process of the products/processes/services.
6. Availability of land, water, electricity, raw materials, manpower, funds required for the production and distribution products/processes/services.

7. Risk perceived and mitigation of risk.
8. Estimated sales and Profitability of business enterprise at least for 5 years.
9. Future business prospects to scale up the business.

After studies of say 3 different ideas and identification of opportunities, the entrepreneur must begin with one business opportunity which is to be done by the next steps called selection of opportunity or validation.

Selection or validation of opportunity involving products/ processes/services [PPS]-

Entrepreneurs should not lose the opportunity to start their enterprise. It is relevant to quote the views of Thomas J. Watson a American businessman and served as CEO of IBM, hereunder.

"Opportunity never knocks on the door; you have to knock on the opportunity's door, and they are all around."

This stage is very critical and entrepreneur and enterprise both should be in one line and length to achieve the success. This process of selection and validation of opportunity is also called the zero-down process.

At this stage, the guidance and support from mentor and subject experts plays a great role.

The process involved preparation of information on the parameters of the identified opportunities [ say 3 opportunities], thereafter data are analysed and interpreted in the free and fair way. The opportunity/product which stood first worked out on an average basis and preferred by the entrepreneur may be selected for validation. Once the product is selected its prototype should be developed and then a market study should be done to ascertain the demand and a trial run is carried out for acceptance of products/processes/services by customers. If the report of the market study regarding the demand of the product and customer feedback is received positive the product is selected and validated.

The products/processes and services finally selected/ validated by the entrepreneur are termed as innovative products/ processes/ services.

Entrepreneurs may note that the development of products/ processes/services by a specific process of ideas generation, from existing ideas or fusion of ideas or development of absolutely new ideas, till completion of the process of selection and validation of ideas, is known as innovation of products/ processes/services and such products/processes and services are known as innovative products/processes and services.

•••

CHAPTER 8

# Emerging Business Opportunities

There are many opportunities for the entrepreneurs in various sectors of economy to start their own enterprises. The following sectors are emerging as a fast-growing sector and creating new business opportunities for the entrepreneurs as per current market trends and the prospects for entrepreneurship in the opinion of author., Entrepreneurs may explore these emerging business opportunities as per there interest and due diligence along with the opportunities in other sectors also as per their objectives.

## 1] Information Technology –

Information technology [IT] is a very big segment which has its implications on entire world. Today every individual as well as existing business and industries across all the sectors are having impact of Information technology which has resulted into tremendous growth of IT sector in entire world. Social media like face book, Instagram, LinkedIn, You Tube, Twitter etc., Health and wellness sector like hospital, gym, Entertainment industry, Banking and finance, Insurance, Sports and Games, Travel and Tourism, Hotel and Hospitality, Food industry, Agriculture and Industries, Ecommerce, Payment platform, Fintech and digital lending platforms and Education sectors gives immense opportunity to develop innovative software or improve existing software to make the things more easy to do by the people which will ultimately result in to increase number of users. Information Technology would be into every sector and have the greater impact on the society at large.

## 2] Artificial intelligence and machine learning [AI/ML]-

The application of AI/ML have been seen widespread to every sector in the past few years and there will be exceptional growth in this segment in next few years with the reflection of value and benefits of this application. The data analysis with the use of AL/ML within the shortest possible time create tremendous value for every organization. The entrepreneurs of technical band of mind can explore the possibilities to develop the products or process, which can embed with the AI/ML technology in the existing processes or operation to create the value for their enterprises with the growth of this sector.

## 3] Robotics -

Robotics is having a bright future prospect of growth as its application is increasing in various sectors like Health, Industries, Agriculture, and many more sectors. It creates more value for the organizations wherever the robotics technology is adopted. Entrepreneurs may search for opportunity for application of robotics in various sectors.

## 4] Drone development and application–

Drone is now being used in various sectors and purposes. For example, it is used for spray of medicines to the agricultural crops, or for survey or sending essential goods in remote places or by military establishment for keeping watch on border of the country. Entrepreneurs may find the opportunity in drone related segment.

## 5] Medical devices-

The health awareness among the people is increasing but the specialized medical services are not easily available particularly in remote areas. This creates the requirement of medical devices like small size ECG machine, small ultrasonography machine, Blood pressure instruments, glucometer etc for want of early diagnosis of diseases and consulting specialist by the health workers or by the people themselves for appropriate treatment even from remote places. Entrepreneurs may explore the possibilities of innovative medical devices keeping in view the need of the people.

### 6] Veterinary devices –

Health of the animals is important from economic point of view for all types of animals. Likewise pet animals also need good health care. Entrepreneurs can explore the possibilities of development of veterinary devices which can keep the watch on the health of animals and if any sign of disease is noticed, the same can be used for consultation and treatment from veterinary doctor.

### 7] E-commerce business –

Ecommerce business is the fastest growing business worldwide. There are many sellers of the same products. The entrepreneurs may explore the possibilities of trading few identified products on online platforms like Amazon and flip cart where they can have enough margin between prize on the online platform and the procurement price in wholesale market or in direct purchase from manufacturers.

### 8] Manufacturing sector-

This sector provides wide scope for entrepreneurs, as it is applicable for every sector of economy where manufacturing process is involved which includes small industries to big industries. Entrepreneurs can develop their own product or new technology or manufacturing process and go for manufacturing of their own products based on that and launch in the market.

### 9] Export business –

Export business is one of the fastest growing businesses in the global economy. This business is having two sections as under. –

1] Export of goods/services to oversees countries.

2] Import of goods/services from the oversees countries.

Most of the entrepreneurs think that the export business is not an easy one because of the various rules and regulations but it's not a truth. In fact, once the entrepreneurs decide to entre in to export business, they will get the support from government agencies, chamber of commerce, Embassies of different countries, Director general of foreign trade and export councils in their efforts to become a exporters and importers Now a days every country is promoting export activities to earn the foreign currency to improve their position of balance of payments. Entrepreneurs can take export import code from Director general of foreign trade to start their export and import business. They can manufacture their identified products or get it manufactured from others and can sale it in domestic as well as oversees market. They can start export activities in joint venture with existing manufacturers. Entrepreneurs in initial stage do this business after ascertaining credentials of buyers in overseas country from exports promotion councils/ embassies or through credit agencies and supply the goods on full payment or against letter of credit of full amount.

### 10] Nutritional products-

Customers are now becoming health conscious and prefer the healthier food and other nutritional products. These products includes nutraceutical products also. In food products categories, people prefer organically grown foods, high fibre contents fruits and vegetables which keeps them physically and mentally healthy and energetic with good immunity to protect them from diseases. Consumers are having good concern about cleanliness as well as the contents of the products. Companies maintaining the required quality standard create their brand value and growing faster than their competitors lacking in quality standard. Some sections of the society prefer the home-made food not only for homely taste but for good quality, which have been cooked with all required cleanliness. This trend of healthy food and wellness products, which are also environmentally friendly, will be widely spread in days to come. Entrepreneurs may explore the business opportunity in this segment in the best of their judgement.

### 11] Lifestyle and fashion products -

Fashion is changing very fast with liking of consumers for the cost effective and environmentally friendly products. For examples people's choice for cosmetics made up from natural ingredients is increasing or in jewellery segment peoples liking for lab grown diamond or in textiles segment peoples liking for comfort in wearing are the new trend. This segment can be a good option for the entrepreneurs.

### 12] Green energy -

Green energy like solar energy, wind energy, and other alternative source of energy which protect our environment are going to boom across the world. The use of the product like e-vehicles will increase because there is no pollution from such vehicle and vehicle running cost is very less. Biofuel is another area which creates opportunity for the entrepreneurs.

### 13] Waste Management -

This segment is a combination of so many vertices like E-waste, plastic and rubber waste, electronic appliances, biodegradable waste, household waste, Agricultural waste, scrap vehicles waste, furniture waste, waste from dismantling of ship or permanently shut down industries etc. Recycling of waste and reuse the extracts from the waste or make the same or other product useful in the economy, creates promising business opportunities for the entrepreneurs.

### 14] Genetic Engineering and Biotechnology -

Application of Genetic Engineering and Biotechnology is in many fields like in plant and animal kingdom, preservation of human or animal's umbilical cells for treatment of serious diseases, regeneration of new body organ, preservation of organs for transplant to save the life etc. This sector is the booming sector, and it will grow many folds in future. Entrepreneurs may explore this sector for business opportunity.

### 15] Organic cultivation –

The awareness about health and wellness has resulted in to increase of organic food products among the people. This provides a great scope in agricultural sector to cultivate the agricultural crops, fruits, vegetables, medicinal plants etc. Entrepreneurs may explore this segment to achieve their objectives.

### 16] Consultancy and professional services-

This segment is fast growing for the reason that that peoples want to hire the services of expert for specific works so that work is done in a precision way and within the shortest possible time. For example, people like to avail the services of Chartered accountant for ensuring that their financial statements are made correctly, and they are fully complied with tax liabilities, or of Architect for the drawing and designing from hotel, home, hospital any other construction projects or of psychologists for mental health or of Lifestyle couch and motivational speakers. The scope is very wide, and entrepreneurs may focus to start consultancy and professional services according to their experience and expertise. The brand or image building is key of success in this segment.

To sum up entrepreneurs may explore the above emerging business opportunities along with the opportunity in the sectors of their preference and select the most beneficial opportunity to start their entrepreneurial journey.

•••

CHAPTER 9

# Establishment of an Enterprise - Basic Steps

To start a business enterprise, the entrepreneur has to constitute a structured organization such as A proprietor ship firm having a proprietor / or partnership firm having minimum two partners or Pvt Ltd company having minimum two director or limited liability partnership having minimum two partner /or public limited company having minimum three directors.

The setting up of an enterprise involves registration of firm/ company and other statutory compliances. The entrepreneurs must connect with the concerned dept./agencies/authorities for applicable procedural requirements. The services of service provider/advisors may be availed for the purpose wherever required to avoid statutory or other lapses and save time. Single point clearance facilities have been set up by concerned governments and the same may be applied. Most of the registration and licenses are required to apply online and it will be granted to you online. We discuss hereunder a brief detail about basic registration procedure of all above constitution of enterprises except public limited as it may require many formalities, and statutory clearance and therefore it should be done as per guidance of experts and company secretary. Here it is further clarified that for all enterprises there are other permission and statutory clearance are required hence it is recommended to seek guidance of your mentor or experts or advisors from time to time so that you are having all statutory registration and clearances.

## Basic Registrations Requirement

| Procedural Requirement | Concerned Office | Remarks |
|---|---|---|
| **Constitution**<br>Proprietorship firm.<br>Partnership firm.<br>Company (Pvt. Ltd.) and limited liability partnership. | State government.<br>Registrar of firms of state of government.<br>Registrar of companies. | Shop establishment registration [Applicable for every enterprise]<br>Registrar of firm.<br>Registrar of company for Incorporation certificate of company /LLP. |
| **Registration**<br>For industry or<br>Ancillary unit. | Dept. of Industries of state government. | Temporary Registration & Permanent Registration before and after establishment of the unit. |
| For good and services tax (State & Central]. | GST dept of state and central government. | GST registration. |
| Patents &Trademark. | Trademark Registry. | Registration of trademark. |
| Food product activity. | Drug and food dept. of state Govt. | FSSAI License. |
| Medicine related activities. | Drug and food dept. of state Govt. | Drug license. |
| Import and export activities. | Director general foreign trade. | Import export registration cum import export code. |
| For water & Air pollution Control. | Pollution Control Board or Authorities. | Clearance or no objection from these authorities, wherever is required. |

In addition to the above there are provisions to obtain registration and clearance from specific dept. to which the nature of your activity relates to such dept. For example, you will require clearance from Rubber board for rubber products and forest clearance for wood products.

Entrepreneurs also require compliance with Taxation regulations enforced from time to time under the guidance of their tax consultants as noncompliance carries fine and penalties as prescribed in TAX LAWS.

The entrepreneur may seek guidance on the issue of statutory clearances as the rules and applicability get changed from time to time.

The above information shall surely help the entrepreneurs to move on to set up their enterprises.

●●●

CHAPTER 10

# Strategic Business Plan Preparation

The strategic planning for the entrepreneur is critical and essential to run the business successfully. The entrepreneur has limited resources in terms of time, finance and manpower. The entrepreneur is going to put his money into starting the venture and without proper planning this investment may come into risk. Entrepreneur expects the business to make reasonable profit and give returns on his investment. The opportunity to be 'your own boss' is part of this return.

It is, therefore, necessary that enterprises select very carefully the fronts for action and formulate all the strategies with due care and calculated risk as the entrepreneur cannot afford to make mistakes which will cost him in terms of time, money, and peace.

## 1. What Is Strategic Planning:

Strategic planning is a preparation of road map with action plan keeping in view the production capacity, availability of resources, funds arrangement, sales target, and goal of the entrepreneur. Business planning also requires proper analysis of the business environment, the products, processes and services, the people involved, the target customers and entrepreneur himself in a certain perspective.

### i. Why The Planning Is Necessary:

Most enterprises are affected by the volatile and competitive market conditions an entrepreneur should plan for aggressive business strategies to compete with the competitor in respect of quality, services, and pricing and at the same time keep proper provision for volatility in the market. Continuous planning and re-planning are necessary to reduce the risk to the great extent.

ii. **Advantage of Strategic Planning for The Entrepreneurs:**

Strategic planning depicts the purpose and right direction to the entrepreneur to enable him to be well informed with status of implementation and running of his business enterprise so that he can make best use of his resources and to take right decision at right time. Strategic planning always has inbuilt priority and time frame for variety of work involved and it makes it easy for the entrepreneur to use his time in line with stipulated priority and ensure to accomplish the work or goal within the prescribed time schedule.

iii. **Strategic Planning and Risk Mitigation:**

The strategic planning will give an idea to the entrepreneur about anticipated risk and accordingly the entrepreneur will take the steps in advance for mitigation of such risk if arises or he can keep his alternative plan [plan B] ready to overcome on such risk which may hampers the implementation and progress of his Enterprise.

## 2. Strategic Planning as Per Types of Entrepreneurships:

Strategic planning to be made as required for the type of entrepreneurship which are discussed in related chapter. Every type of entrepreneurship has some or other role of computer system, internet, online sales, e-commerce, and other technology, and same should find a place in the planning. Likewise planning should be made keeping in view available resources, fund position, backward and forward linkages Goal, targeted sales and profit, budget provisions and factors which may affect achievement of goal.

The planning need not be complex, rather it should be clear, simple and easy to understand and implemented. For example, the sales target should be fixed considering the demand for the product or services and depending on that production targets are fixed but with cross verification of resources available and production capacity. In the same way planning should give due importance to external factors like change in policy by regulator, people preference, market condition and competition. The goal for entrepreneur is to earn the profit with mitigation of risk involved.

### 3. Periodical Review of Actual Progress Against the Estimation Made in The Plan:

Strategic plans should be reviewed, and actual achievement should be compared with estimations from the management information system [MIS], periodic returns, and feedback from concerned officials. If there is a gap between actual performance and estimation, the entrepreneur should examine the reason and take necessary steps to remove the hurdles/shortcomings if any at the earliest possible and decides further course of action.

To sum up, entrepreneurs should give due importance to strategic planning for their successful entrepreneurial journey.

•••

CHAPTER 11

# Basics of Balance Sheet and Profit & Loss Account

Every entrepreneur, irrespective of his educational background, expertise and experience is supposed to know to read the balance sheet and profit & loss account. These are also termed as final accounts and some time as annual financial statements of any enterprise. If an enterprise has a sales turnover above the cut off limit, the balance sheet and profit and loss account [BSPL] are required to be audited by the chartered accountant for genuineness of underlying transactions as per rules and regulations. The audited BSPL are accepted by tax authorities to arrive at total income, taxable income, and tax liability. The BSPL are basic documents asked by the investors, venture capital funds, and bankers for study of the financial health of the enterprise and based on that and other factors, they take the decision for providing the funds for the project.

The profit and loss account indicates the operational result of the enterprise and shows the related transaction of an entire financial year, whereas the Balance sheet reflects the financial position of the enterprise on the specific date. These documents are finalized from the data available in trial balance of the enterprise in which all financial transactions are recorded daily.

We sincerely advise the entrepreneurs to carefully select the competent and experienced account to look after the accounting aspects as well as to handle the taxation part of the enterprise, so that the entrepreneurs can focus on the business development for the growth of the enterprise.

The process of preparation of the above final accounts is explained here under.

## 1. Profit and Loss Account

The Profit and Loss Account, as the name suggests, is prepared to know whether the enterprise has made a profit or booked the loss during a financial year or the period for which the profit and loss is to be calculated. All entries of nominal accounts will be posted into Profit and Loss Account. As an accounting rule, the debit side of P&L account is for posting of all expenses and losses, whereas credit side of P&L account is for posting of all incomes and gains. The totals of the debit entries and credit entries when accounted with each other will arrive at profit or loss made by the enterprise during the financial year or the period for which profit, and loss is to be calculated. If the credit amount is more than debit amount the net result is the profit and debit amount is more than credit amount the net result is loss. Finally, whatever the profit or loss booked by the enterprise; it shall be carried over to the respective balance sheet accounts.

After completing the above postings, the trading account which is the first part of the Profit and Loss Account is prepared. The trading account consists of opening stock, purchases, closing stock, sales, other income like interest on deposit, returns of goods and direct expenses relating to the purchase. Thereafter the next part of PL account is prepared which shows gross profit, all expenses, depreciation, interest, profit before tax, non-operating expenses, income tax and net profit after tax.

## A Typical P&L Shall Appear as Under:

| M/S Ocean enterprises<br>Trading & Profit & Loss Account | | | |
|---|---|---|---|
| **(For the period from April 2022 to March 2023)**<br>**[INR In Lakhs]** | | | |
| **Debit** | | **Credit** | |
| Particulars | Amount | Particulars | Amount |
| Opening stock | 100 | Sales revenue | 250 |
| purchase | 200 | Closing stock | 100 |
| Gross profit [GP] | 50 | | |
| Total | 350 | | 350 |
| GP brought forward | | | 50 |
| Salary and wages | 5 | | |
| water and electricity | 5 | | |
| depreciation | 5 | | |
| Administrative expenses | 5 | | |
| Interest | 5 | | |
| Profit before tax | | | 25 |
| Income tax | 5 | | |
| Net profit after tax | | | 20 |

### Balance Sheet

After preparation of the Profit & Loss Account, the next step is to prepare the Balance Sheet to know the financial position of the enterprise on a particular date. The Balance Sheet shows on the left side the liabilities of the enterprise and on the right side it shows the assets of the enterprise.

Now to prepare the balance sheet all personal and real accounts will appear on the Balance Sheet. The assets side will consist of accounts having debit balances and, on the liabilities, side will consist of accounts having credit balances. Thereafter all assets and liabilities will be posted in respective head in the Balance Sheet. The total assets and total liabilities of the balance sheet should match each other. In case both the sides of balance sheet do not tally with each other, that means some mistake is happened in the books of accounts and it requires finding out the mistake and correction of the same.

## A Typical Balance Sheet Shall Appear as Under:

| M/S Ocean enterprises<br>Balance Sheet<br>[As on 31st March 2023]<br>[INR IN LAKHS] | | | | | |
|---|---|---|---|---|---|
| **Liabilities** | | **INR** | **Assets** | | **INR** |
| Capital | | 100 | Land and building | | 50 |
| Reserve and surplus | 20 | 20 | Plant and machinery | | 40 |
| Add profit. | 10 | | Total fixed assets. | | 90 |
| Less drawing | 10 | | Non-current assets | | 30 |
| Unsecured loan | | 20 | Current assets | | 100 |
| Secured term loan | | 30 | Inventory | 50 | |
| Current liabilities | | 50 | Receivables | 30 | |
| Sundry creditors | 20 | | Advance to customers | 15 | |
| Short term loan/ working capital limit. | 30 | | Cash and bank balance | 5 | |
| **TOTAL** | | **220** | **Total** | | **220** |

Analysis of Final statements- Financial analysis of financial statements is necessary to arrive at a decision whether the financial position of the enterprise is strong, good, satisfactory, or bad. For this purpose, an interrelationship between the balance sheet figures and between the P&L figures is worked out. This exercise is called ratio analysis.

The following important ratio are being discussed here:

1. **Total Outside Liabilities to Tangible Net Worth= TOL/ TNW**

   Here TOL consists of all term liabilities such as secured and unsecured loans and all current liabilities. The tangible net worth consists of capital +reserve and surplus = less intangible like good-will, patents etc.

   This ratio gives an idea of how many times of TNW, the total liability is there, on the enterprise. Say the ratio 4:1 means TOL is 4 against TNW 1. If this ratio is up to 4 1is considered good but above that it is not considered a good ratio.

2. **Debt to equity-** Debt to equity ratio is the same as TOL/ TNW. Here debt means total outside liabilities and equity means TNW.

3. **Current Ratio** – This is the ratio of current assets [CA] to current liabilities [CL]. = CA/CL. Current assets mean those assets which can be converted into cash in one year and current liabilities are those liabilities which are payable within the next year. The current ratio of 1.33:1 is considered a benchmark ratio which shows that current assets are 1.33 against current liability of 1, and therefore current liability can be paid from current assets easily.

4. **Net profit to net sales ratio** - This is the ratio of net profit to net sales, and it is expressed in percentage terms. = net profit/net sales =x 100.

Suppose the value comes to 10% means the net profit is 10 percent of sales revenue and it is considered good. Net profit to net sales below 10 % needs the strategy to improve the same.

To sum up, the balance sheet and profit and loss account are the backbones of an enterprise, and entrepreneurs should always keep their eyes on the figures that appear therein and study the corresponding statistics, sales, and profit and keep watch on receivables and payables account and wherever necessary take the corrective action.

•••

CHAPTER 12

# Preparation of Project Report

Project report is a comprehensive document in which all the aspects of business enterprises [hereinafter referred to as "project"] are incorporated. It covers precisely technical feasibility and economic/financial viability of the project. It gives a fair idea about the project viability not only to the entrepreneur but also to investor and bankers and thus become a most useful document for raising funds for the business enterprise.

The important points to be covered in the Project are given here in below, based on which a fair idea of preparation of project report can be drawn. In case an entrepreneur does not have basic financial knowledge, he may provide the required details to any competent financial consultant and get it prepared.

The project report discussed the entire gambit of the project in two sections.

1. Promoter
2. Project

**Promoter:**

This part covers all the information about the promoter.

i. **General Information** - Name, Age, address, contact details. PAN no. Aadhar card no. educational qualification, training, experience, and expertise.

ii. **Character** - This covers his general behaviour and financial behaviour.

iii. **Competency** [knowledge +skill]

iv. **Capital** - How much total capital or net worth of the promoter and of which how much liquid capital he is having to invest in his business.

v. **Capability** - This covers his capabilities to run the business successfully.

**Project Covers the Following Aspects:**

i. Name of business enterprises, address of registered office. Corporate office and factories, PAN no., GST no., contact details.

ii. Constitution like Proprietorship firm, Partnership firm. Limited liability partnership, Pvt Ltd or Public Ltd company, Trust or Society etc., Date of establishment etc. Details of required statutory registration/ certificate or clearances obtained.

iii. Project in brief, specifying the type of project like business/ manufacturing/ services, Name of product, which is going to be manufactured, Demand and supply position of the product, Market competition, risk involved and how the same will be mitigated, how much sales and profit is expected and what are long term prospects.

iv. Cost of project comprising of cost of land, cost of construction, or cost of ready built premises, Cost of plant and machinery, preliminary and post operative expenses etc. working capital required.

v. Assessment of working capital requirement for the project.

vi. Means of Finance mainly comprises of promoters' contribution, unsecured loans from friends and relatives, and credit facilities from bank or financial institutions by way of term loan for capital expenses and cash credit facility for working capital requirement.

vii. Assumption made in the project like Total capacity, capacity utilization, implementation period, commercial operation date, cost of inputs, Sale price of the product, number of days of credit to be given on sales and number of credit days credit available on purchase etc.

viii. Technical feasibility of the project – The techno-viability study is done to arrive at the availability of all backward and forward linkages necessary for success of the project. It covers brief description of availability of land, or building and its suitability for the project, Availability of water, electricity, manpower, Plant and machinery, technology, raw materials, transportation etc at reasonable cost and marketing of the product with details of demand and supply position and sales model like online sales and/or distributor or franchisee sales model etc.

ix. Financial Viability – To arrive at the financial viability of a project, a detailed study is to be done. For that purpose, projected balance sheet and profit and loss account [here in after called "financials"] for next five years is to be prepared. The project will be judged on various financial parameters such as breakeven analysis and the various key ratio like Debt coverage ratio, current ratio, Debt equity ratio, profitability ratio, benefit coast ratio and internal rate of return which are to be calculated based on the financial statements mentioned above. Sensitivity analysis is also to be done considering a certain percentage of decline in sales or increase in cost of inputs and its effects on all the above financial parameters. If all the above financial parameter shows that project is profitable and shows that profit will be sufficient to service the loan if any to be availed and leave sufficient balance of the profit with the enterprises and entrepreneur, the project is considered as financially viable.

WHEN THE PROJECT IS JUDGED AS TECHNICALLY FEASIBLE AND FINANCIALY VIABLE IT CAN BE TAKEN UP FOR IMPLIMENTAION

x. Project Implementation Schedule – This covers every aspect from the beginning of the project till commercial production is started. Like date of applying for license, statutory registrations, date of acquiring premises, date of completion of construction [if required], date of ordering plant and machinery, date of installation of plant and machinery, date of purchase of inventory, date of commercial operation.

xi. Bank Loan Sanction and Draw Down Schedule - This schedule should cover Name of bank, date for submission of application for credit facilities to bank, date of sanction [estimated if not sanction], draw down date and amount for term loan, date of availment for working capital. The draw down for term loan should be matches with payment to vendors/suppliers for capital assets.

To sum up, we would impress upon the entrepreneur to start an entrepreneurial journey with confidence once your project report says that your project is technically feasible and financially viable.

•••

CHAPTER 13

# Project Appraisal

The project appraisal is evaluation of the project to a certain the viability of the project. The project is appraised by way of detailed analysis of various aspects of the project.

1. Technical Feasibility.
2. Economic Viability.
3. Financial Viability.
4. Marketing Analysis.
5. Managerial Efficiency.

## Technical Feasibility:

Entrepreneurs are supposed to study whether the product can be manufactured or kind of services to be launched is practically and technically possible and whether it can be given a shape of fully functional and profitable venture with available technology, plant and machinery, equipment, manpower and other necessary resources.

Precisely technical feasibility means to evaluate the availability of resources and the capacity and technology used in the proposed plant and machinery and equipment to produce the product or developed the services within the time schedule.

Once the entrepreneurs get convinced that the project can be taken up and made a functional and profitable venture, they can move ahead to create the needed facilities. While selected the P&M

and equipment, it is essential that the technical specifications of P&M and equipment should be properly studied and compared with the technology and technical specifications used in other plants & machinery available in the market to produce similar kinds of products. The know-how, technology used, and initial training to operate are important aspect of high-tech P&M and equipment hence it should be ascertained that whether the manufacturer or their supplier shall provide the above-mentioned support to the entrepreneurs. Entrepreneurs should compare the cost, warranties, and after-sales service aspect and whatever the better option comes, that kind of P&M and equipment should be selected. The arrangement made to procure the P&M and equipment should be examined. If the project is proposed to be implemented in collaboration with other local or foreign companies in that situation, collaboration agreement should be executed with detailed terms and conditions, giving respect to applicable laws.

The other aspect for evaluating the technical feasibility of the project is as under.

i. Location of project and its connectivity with nearby cities and transport hubs.

ii. Availability of land, topography of land, land is developed, or it require land development, if so what kind of work to be carried out to develop the land and cost involved.

iii. Availability of facilities like water, power, logistic and transport, sewage line, water treatment plant, sewage treatment plant, telephonic and internet facilities.

iv. Availability of service facilities like machine shops, fabrication units, electric repair shop, online common service centres, postal and courier services and printing and stationery.

v. Availability of skilled, semi-skilled and unskilled workers and arrangements to impart the training to such workers in different trades.

vi. Availability of raw material, and consumables in required quantity and quality.

## Economic Viability:

Economic viability is the macro-economic impact of the project on society and environment as a whole and on the entrepreneurs. The project is said to be economically viable when economic benefit exceeds the economic cost of the project. The project may have a positive impact on the life of a person not connected directly with the project. The revenue generated from the project may be less than the actual benefit it gives to society. For example, a good nicely built road project may benefit in terms of speed, saving fuel and time by paying a small amount of toll tax. It is important to analyse that the project and its location is in fine tuning with Government policies on industrialization and environmental policies and whether it is entitles for government incentives, grant in aid etc. which may directly affect the project cost to be meet out by the entrepreneur. There are some more aspects of economic viability such as analysis of required raw materials, installed capacity, estimated capacity utilization, sales, expenses, and profits. Demand for the product to be carefully studied as it will directly impact on the achievement of estimated sales and ultimately earnings from the project.

## Financial Viability:

The financial viability of the project is analysis of requirement of funds, means of finance, estimated and projected sales and profitability of the project. In any project the first thing that is required is the arrangement of finance, being the main input of the project, which brings all the backward and forward linkages together. Therefore, entrepreneurs must analyse financial viability in all its aspects as discussed here under.

1. **Project Cost** - As a first step item wise assessment of the cost for fixed assets, such as land, building, plant and machinery, equipment, installation of plant and machinery, electrification, furniture, and fixture, are to be made. The pre operating and post operative expenses and interest during the moratorium period [if the bank loan is to be availed] shall also to be included in the project cost. The margin required for working capital may be considered as part of project cost, but it should come from promoter's contribution to the extent of 100%.

2. **Means Of Finance** – Means of finance will be 25% of promoter's contribution on capital cost and 75% will be financed from banks as a term loan in normal course. The entire working capital margin shall come from the promoter's contribution.

   The entrepreneurs should carefully analyse each item of project cost to consider it for the project.

3. **Working Capital Finance** - The working capital finance is that amount of funds which are required for one working capital cycle or operating cycle of the enterprise. It starts from cash which will be used to purchase the raw material [RM] and then it will be converted to finished goods [FG]which will sold in cash and the cycle is completed but some time FG is sold in credit, and it becomes receivables, when receivables get realized it will again convert into cash. This working capital cycle goes on and on. To continue the working capital cycle the adequate of working capital is must to continue the business operation. The proper assessment of working capital is discussed in the chapter on working capital Management.

4. The profitability of the project is the most important pillar. The estimated financial statements [FS] such as balance sheet and profit and loss account are prepared for the next 5 years. The FS are analysed on various financial parameters and ratio of which some important parameters are explained here under.

i. **Breakeven Point** - Every unit has the installed capacity, but capacity utilization may be less. This BE point will indicate that on which level sales value and cost will be equal. If BE point is lower, better is the project financial viability. In other words, on BE point there will be no profit or no loss situation. In a separate chapter breakeven analysis is discussed in detail.

ii. **Net Present Value** [NPV] - This indicates what is the present value of future income. It is calculated by discounting of cost and benefits by discounting factor at the desired rate of return [IRR] which is considered viable. In general, 15% IRR is considered viable. After discounting cost and benefit for each year till life of the assets [usually up to 9 years] or repayment tenor, and thereafter sum of each year NPV is calculated for all years. If NPV of benefits is more than NPA of cost, it's called Positive NPV. Means the project is financially viable.

iii. **Benefit Cost Ratio** - When NPV of benefits divided by NPV of cost and the value come more than 1, the project is considered as financially viable.

iv. **Internal Rate of Return** [IRR] - The IRR of the project indicates at what rate at which the investment is return by calculating the present value of investments and future receipts. It is a rate of return received on the investment made in the project. If the IRR is more than

15% the project is considered financially viable. It can be calculated on easy templates available online.

v. **Debt Service Coverage Ratio** [DSCR] – If the term loans are to be availed from bank or any financial institutions, a good average DSCR makes the proposal good for the finance. It is the ratio of amount of cash profit and the liability of term loan instalment and interest. Simple formula is Profit after tax + depreciation + interest on term loan/ term loan instalment during the year + interest on term loan. The average DSCR should minimum 1.5:1

vi. **Net Profit Ratio** – Net profit ratio is calculated in terms of net sales. Its calculation is done as per formula - Net Profit/Net sales = x 100= It gives net profit %. If this net profit comes to around 10 %, it is considered a good profit.

vii. **Return On Capital Employed Ratio** [ROCE] – It is calculated to know what is return on capital employed in the project. It calculated with the help of formula – EBIT/ Capital employed [ here EBIT is earning before interest and tax and capital employed is total assets -current liabilities], the value then multiplied by 100 to express it in percentage.

viii. **Other Important Ratios** - There are some other important ratios like D/E ratio, current ratio etc. which all should be within the acceptable range to consider the proposal as financially viable. These ratios are explained in the chapter on balance sheet and profit and loss account.

The financial analysis to arrive at financial viability of a project require the sound knowledge of finance, it is therefore advised that the entrepreneur may avail the services of subject expert and once it adjudged that project is financially viable, he may move ahead with further analysis of project in respect of other points.

## Marketing Analysis:

Entrepreneurs are expected to do market research and identify the market as well as customers segment for their products. Success of entrepreneurs ultimately comes from the sale of the product to the customers in the identified market. It is therefore important to analyse the market where the product is having demand for sale to the customers. If the entrepreneurs are satisfied with the demand in the selected market to achieve the estimated sales, the project is treated as viable from the marketing aspect. The marketing aspect is discussed in a separate chapter of this book for the knowledge of the entrepreneurs.

## Managerial Appraisal:

It is a proven fact that management competency is an essential element in making a successful enterprise. Because of such a prime importance of managerial competence in the success of enterprise the investors or bankers also look for managerial qualities in the entrepreneur before putting their money in to the projects. Many times, good project fails which are otherwise feasible because of lack of managerial qualities and a poor project may register a success with good managerial qualities. The entrepreneur should carefully select the employees in the management cadre who have managerial qualities and lead the team as leader. The entrepreneur himself should also develop all the qualities of highly successful managers and thought leaders to run the business successfully. If an honest entrepreneur is satisfied with his own managerial competency and qualities of thought leader, he may move on to take up the project confidently.

It's advisable that for highly technical projects the entrepreneur should engage the competent consultancy company to conduct techno-economic viability [TEV] study of the project and if in TEV study the project viability is confirmed, the project may be selected for implementation.

To sum up, Entrepreneurs should carefully appraise the project on all the above points, and if it is found that the project is technically feasible and financially viable and finding regarding other aspects of project appraisal are also positive, the project will surely be successful venture.

•••

CHAPTER 14

# Intellectual Property Rights [IPR]

IPR means the legal monopoly of the creator of the class of the property or products or processes. Such properties, products, or processes [IP] come into existence because of the application of human intellect or mind of the creator. Therefore, the creators have legal rights on their IP, and they should be legally protected from infringement or stealing of their IP. That means without prior permission of the creator no one can use his/her creation. IPR have made applicable in India and many other countries when world trade organization came into existence in the year 1995. The IPR gives protection from infringement or stealing for different periods to the innovator depending on the category in which the IPR registered and rules of the countries where the IPR registered. In the WTO, agreement the trade related intellectual property rights [TRIPS] covers the different form of IPR, like Patents, copy rights, trademarks, new plant variety, integrated circuits, Industrial designs, etc. Some of them are discussed here under-.

## 1] Patents. -

Patent is the right of the innovator granted by the concerned government offices, for their creativity and intellect, for limited period, by way of exclusive rights to the innovator, to make, use, exercise, and sale their products and process made by them as per their IP. Like other property, the patents being an exclusive right can be sold, licensed, transferred or willed to other interested party. Patents can also be offered as collateral like their other assets. The patent can be classified in to 3 categories as follows. -

i] **Utility patents** – It broadly covers the following innovations-

[a] Processes- It covers innovations in development and application of new technology or improvement in existing processes of production, testing, research, analysis etc.

[b] Machines - It covers innovation of advance plant and machineries to produce the high-quality products in bigger quantity with high installed capacity and advance instruments to give quick and accurate results and sophisticated equipment to make the production process smooth and easy.

[c] Manufacturer - It covers the application of innovation of machinery and process into the manufacturing of products.

[d] Composition of matter – It covers the new chemical, medicinal or pharmaceutical or nutraceutical or other chemical products, having better use for the peoples and which are not grown naturally.

ii] **Design patents** – It covers the innovative ornamental design of articles like jewellery, shoes, clothing, bicycle, which is a part of shape or configuration of an object and cannot be separated from it. This type of patent protects only the outside appearance of the product. If the innovators want to protect the inner structure and functionality, they must file utility patents.

iii] **Plant patents** – It protects the new and distinctive variety of plants. The plant should be asexually produced by cutting or grafting and it should not be produced by seed or by tuber propagation. Such a plant should not exist in an uncultivated state or grow naturally.

The utility and design patents can be filed in India as well as in many other countries wherever provision exist. There is no provision of plant patent in India but innovators if they want can file in the countries where such provision exist.

## Eligibility criteria-

The eligibility criteria for applying for Patent are as under –

i] Genuinely true and first innovator himself.

ii] Assignee of genuinely true and first innovator, having right to make such application on behalf of genuinely true and first innovator.

iii] Legal representative of expired genuinely true and first innovator, who was eligible for such application before he or she expired.

## 2] Trademarks. –

The trademark is any mark by name, or symbol, or image or word, phrase, which differentiates the products made or sold by one entity from the products manufactured by others. The trademark IPR is registered for the initial period of 10 years and thereafter it can be renewed every 10 years till the products are manufactured or sold by the entity. It gives the support to the entity to position the product in the market and customers get assured about the quality of the product. The registered trademark is always distinctive and deceptive of similarity. Copying of other trademarks makes the person liable for legal action. Trademarks are useful in brand building, but trademarks may be a small part of the brand whereas brand refers to an overall image of the company and therefore it may include trademark and things like logo, customers feel good reactions etc. Branding the business is one of the essential parts to win the loyalty of the customers. The entrepreneurs must obtain the trademark for their products to get the legal protection against copying their product and at the same time build the brand and brand image of their enterprise to make the loyal customers by making quality products available to them.

### 3] Industrial designs-

The industrial design registration protects the unique look of the product or articles. The protection of registered owner is available against the visual features termed as design which comprises of shape, pattern, and ornamental appearance or combination of any two of these features.

### 4] Copy rights. –

Copyrights relates to protection of creative work of the creator in relation to art and culture like literacy, music, films, plays or drama etc. However, a person having the copyright can authorize others to use the copyright items as per his own discretion. It may be noted that there is no copyright on an idea or concept if the idea or concept is used in a different way. Likewise, there is no copyright on transmission of live events.

### 5] Integrated circuits-

The integrated circuit registration comes under IPR and protects the chip design and material used to develop the integrated circuit. In India it is protected under Semiconductor integrated circuit layout design [SICLD] Act2000. Innovators can make commercial use of their innovation and have legal protection in case of any infringement noticed by them.

To sum up, the entrepreneurs should take protection as per intellectual property rights by patent and trademark registration of their product/process as per provision of law and register for protection of integrated circuit, plant patents, designs, or any other required protection available and applicable in your case.

•••

CHAPTER 15

# Fund Raising for Finance to Entrepreneurs and Startup Enterprises.

Funds requirements start from the start of startup entrepreneurial journey, fund requirements are always a purpose driven which are given here under-.

1. Market research and idea creation.
2. Validation of ideas and Prototype development.
3. Statutory registrations, licenses, and clearances.
4. Product development.
5. Appointment of suitable employees.
6. Purchase of land and factory building or shed and office expenses.
7. Purchase of plant and machinery and equipment.
8. Working capital of one operating cycle including administrative, marketing and sales expenses.

**Sources of Funding:**

1. **At First Stage or Market research and idea creation Stage:**

   At this stage outside funding is not available to entrepreneurs and they must arrange the funds from their own sources.

2. **At Second Stage or Seed Stage:**

   Validation of ideas and Prototype development. At this stage, the prototype is ready, and entrepreneurs move ahead to conduct the market study and do the trial run to ascertain the demand of product/process or services usually referred as proof of concept [POC]. At this stage the entrepreneurs need the fund to engage the mentor and create the team of employees, formation of business entities, obtaining statutory licenses, certificates and clearances, business plan preparation with estimated balance sheet and P&L account for 3 years and estimated profitability statement for proposed repayment period, detailed project report preparation, Techno economic viability [if required], thereafter initiate the process for office and factory set up. For all the above purposes funding shall be required. At this stage funding shall be available from following –

   i. **Incubators** – Incubators work is mostly delegated to reputable institutions and universities where a separate incubation cell is created to assist the entrepreneurs from validation of concept to launching of the product. These incubators hold the hands of entrepreneurs and guide them from time to time. They provide the funds in the shape of grant and the debt to meet the fund requirement of the enterprise.

   ii. **Seed Fund Scheme** – Government has created the seed funds and they are managed by well-known public sector financial institutions. These funds provide seed capital to the entrepreneurs at very low interest rates and without any collateral security.

   iii. **Angel Investors** – These are private investors, and they invest in equity in the startup having potential of fast growth and create value on their investment.

The entrepreneur needs to pitch desk of their project in brief covering all the points, especially the future out looks to the investors in some conference, on video or in person and submit a detailed proposal to them and convince them to make the investment. Entrepreneurs having good proposals will surely get the investment from angel investors.

iv. **Crowd Funding** – This refers to funding of small amount from so many people by online crowd funding platforms. This kind of funding may contribute the funds for some promising projects but for most small projects the fund collection in this mode is always a challenging task.

3. **At Third Stage or Operational Stage:**

At this stage factory and office set up is completed, commercial production is started, distributors, dealers and stockiest are appointed and product/process and services launched in the market identified by the entrepreneurs, and business must start at full swing. At this stage major fund requirement arises. The following sources provide funding at this stage.

i. **Venture Capital Funds** – These funds are set up with the intention of making an investment by way of equity participation, having potential for high growth, a bright future outlook and creating value for their investment in a short span of time. These funds extend their support as a mentor to the enterprise once they make investment in it.

ii. **Venture Debt Fund** - These types of funds provide private investment by way of debt generally along with venture capital fund or angel investors but exceptionally without a participation of venture capital fund or angel investors. The debt raised by this mode will be the interest bearing and repayable as per terms and condition mutually agreed by the debt fund and entrepreneurs.

iii. **Banks, Non-Banking Finance Company [NBFC], And Financial Institutions:**

Banks and financial institutions are having a proactive approach in funding start up entrepreneurs. Entrepreneurs need to submit a well drafted credit proposal to the bank along with the project reports, all statutory clearances, and other documents as per the requirement of the bank. Banks provide the funding by way of term loan for creation of fixed assets and repayable in 5-7 years depending on profit generation and working capital limit for one working capital cycle as running credit facility, bills discounting facilities, export finance by way of pre shipment and post shipment credit and non-fund-based facilities like letter of credit and bank guarantee. NBFC provides term loans only. The Financial institutions set up under government support are also provide term loan only.

The details of various credit facilities available from the Banks are given in the Chapter on Banking in this book.

iv. **CSR Funds:**

Many big companies have huge CSR funds, such CSR funds are created for the purpose of social causes. If the products/process/services are for the benefit of society at large or for benefit of poor section of society, women's and child development, care of old age people, resolving some environmental issues etc., the CSR fund may provide grant in aid to such start up enterprises.

4. **At Fourth Stage or Scale Up Stage:**

   This is the stage at which business shall start growing fast and achieve a new milestone. At this stage venture capital funds, and some private equity or investment fund may invest in fast growing start-up enterprises. Banks will also consider enhancement in working capital limits, in line with business growth.

5. **At Fifth Stage or Large Scale Expansion or Exit Option Stage:**

   We may discuss the above stage in the following points-

   i. **Merger or acquisition** - At this stage startup entrepreneurs will acquire or merge some entity and make their company a big company with the growth of business many folds OR they may choose to sell their shares and merge their company with another company provided they gets a good valuation of their company.

   ii. **Initial Public Offer [IPO]:**

   The promoter may dilute their equity and go for public offer, at the book value of shares or at a premium as decided in consultation with manager of issue of shares and get the funds from the public to expand the business of the company. The shares will get listed on the stock exchange and traded in the market.

   iii. **Liquidation or pledge of shares by promoters:**

   This is one of the ways of funds arrangement in which promoters dilute their equity and sell their shares to venture capital funds or investment funds. Alternatively, the promoter may pledge the shares to banks or NBFC and raise the loan to meet their financial needs.

iv. **Issue of Debentures:**

The entrepreneurs in their company may raise funds by issue of debenture. These are debt instruments, and they may be convertible into shares or non-convertible debentures payable at maturity. However, interest may be paid as per prospectus of issued at the time of issue of non-convertible debentures.

To sum up, various fundraising resources are available to entrepreneurs. To explore the appropriate resource for fundraising, the entrepreneurs should assess the stage-wise fund's requirement, select one or more investors or funds providers, and, if required, a bank or NBFC. They will require to prepare a good pitch deck and quality proposal for investors or a credit proposal for banks or NBFCs to raise funds for their enterprises.

•••

CHAPTER 16

# Business Growth, Product Diversification and Expansion

There are several ways to start or grow your business. Whatever the options available, an entrepreneur sitting down to make decisions should consider the best options that align with their primary goals.

The purpose of this section is to first understand some important business growth strategies. The list is indicative and not exhaustive and is for informational purposes only.

Some ideas of how to expand or grow your business, among other options. Some possible growth strategies are enumerated below.

The one of the classic growth strategies models is combination of Products and Markets, which is as under:

1. Market penetration.
2. Market development.
3. Product development.
4. Diversification.

## Market Penetration:

This strategy means the company aims to sell more of its existing products in the markets where it already operates but at the same time it reaches up to wider public. This will not require us to put more burden on resources and effort on sales and marketing to drive increased revenue. In this way, the company is trying to increase its market share. In general, this may seem somewhat less risky as the company already trades in the same markets and products, but there may be limits to the growth that can be achieved with this strategy.

### Market Development:

This existing product/new market strategy occurs when a company decides to sell an existing product in a new geographic market. For example, it may mean selling existing products into new international markets, or into new territory of the domestic market. In this model the company has to spend on sales and marketing to reach new consumers of new market to purchase its products/services.

### Product Development:

On the other hand, this strategy requires the development of new products or modification with or without betterment in quality to be sold in existing markets. This can be considered a very common process as companies cannot rely on the same single product range to maintain their presence and growth. In the consumer goods retail industry, companies stay in touch with consumers and innovate their product lines in competitive ways to keep up with specific trends, market needs/ customer's preferences, etc. Developing new products/making modification in existing products, which meet consumer needs requires a thorough understanding of market trends.

### Diversification:

Diversification is often seen as a risky strategy when a company develop and sells a new product/or product range to all together new class of customers and in new domestic and/or overseas markets. The reasons behind such business strategies may be increasing opportunities identified by the company and relied on such new business opportunities of growth for the company. This seems a risky approach compared to other approaches, and therefore the company needs to carefully assess its capabilities before jumping into new products and new territory, regardless of its expertise in conducting their business successfully.

## Franchisee Business Model:

Entrepreneurs may appoint Franchisee for the specific territory is viable options for business growth. In this model, the entrepreneur shares proven ways to build the business to his franchisee in the as per approved business plan of their company to run their business effectively. The franchisee then appoints the dealers and distributors to cover the entire territory. In this model stock and are remain in the books of franchiser and all expenses including marketing shall be also to be borne by franchiser. The franchise shall get the commission for the business he does from his end. The franchisee and franchiser shall enter into the written contract specifying terms and conditions agreed mutually which will legally bind both the parties.

Export business- In the present era the global market is open up to every business subject to compliance with certain rules and regulations of the buyer and seller country. Entrepreneurs may explore the oversees market to sale their products easily. There are export promotion councils who promote exports. The government also promotes export and gives many facilities to the exporters. Entrepreneurs will require an export import code from the director general of foreign trade. Once this is done, he can find out the customers in oversees country from various business councils/ Embassy of importer's country. After finding out the customer and if he is ready to purchase the goods, the Entrepreneur may contact the clearing, freight and forwarding agent and ascertain the cost of export depending on where the goods are delivered. At this stage, an entrepreneur may quote the price of his goods and mention the freight, clearing and forwarding charges if it is to be borne by an exporter entrepreneur. Entrepreneurs must explore the possibilities to start selling their products in the international market for their higher sales and higher profit margin.

## Selling of the Products on Online Platform of E. Commerce Companies:

This is another very good opportunity for entrepreneurs to sale their products on online platforms of E. Commerce companies like Amazon and Flip cart and other e commerce companies OR entrepreneurs themselves can create their own website. This will open up the market in the entire country when the entrepreneur's sale their products online. Here another advantage is that there are no credit sales in this model and entrepreneurs will get the sale proceeds within the period fixed by the online platform prompter company. Entrepreneurs can run their advertisement or marketing campaign to establish their brand and increase the growth in sales turnover and profit. Entrepreneurs while selling on online flatform can explore the possibilities of selling products which are manufactured by other companies by purchasing the products wholesale or directly purchasing from the manufacturer. They can even arrange the products to directly send to facility centres of E commerce companies like amazon facility centre, who will store the products and dispatch the same to the customers when they receive the order. Some precautions are required in trading on E commerce platforms for new entrepreneurs who simply want to start trading activity on Ecommerce platform.

1. Products should be selected carefully after studying bestselling products, difference of price of the product if purchased from manufacturer in bulk and its selling price on Ecommerce platform. Also Work out the packing, advertising, and selling expenses and then calculate the profit. Entrepreneurs may select such products which give at least 15% net profit.

2. After selection of product list, the product on Ecommerce platform. In the beginning start the business from 1 to

3 products and thereafter you may increase to more products.

3. The key word selection should be such that when a customer searches the product, your product should come in upper level of products displayed by the online platform.
4. You should mention description of the products in such a manner that after reading the description by customers, the customers make up their mind to buy the same.
5. The photograph of the product should be from all the angles and the photoshoot of the product preferably should be done by professionals as the customer purchases the products on seeing the products in images only.
6. The packaging of the products should be attractive and as per trend in the market for similar products keeping in view the choice of consumers.
7. Products should not be from the category like electronics where big players are there and also the categories in which return of products are more due to sizes or colours like textiles, readymade dresses etc.
8. The product should not be heavy, say more than 3 kg in weight, otherwise it carries the delivery charges more.
9. The products should be in the reasonable price range say between INR 500 TO INR 5000, as too lower range may not be much profitable due to selling expenses and too high price item will require more funds to purchase in the beginning in bulk from the manufacturer.
10. Entrepreneurs should create their own brand and logo. They can also get their brand registered with the concerned authority.

The above precautions are necessary for entrepreneurs who are beginners, but they can expand their online business and add more and more products once they get the experience.

## Merger and Acquisition:

Mergers refer to the situation when two or more enterprises combine or merge into one enterprise whereas in acquisition one enterprise is acquired by another enterprise. The merger and acquisition by and large convey the same meaning and therefore the same are narrated together. Now a days for mergers and action use of takeover is more frequently used in business circles. This is the common business strategy now a days to expand the business. Some of the benefits are as below.

1. It increases the growth of the organization, the customers of the merged entity also become the customers of the entity in which the other entity is merged.
2. It will help in the diversification of products and new markets will be open up.
3. The size of the balance sheet increased with increase in capital, topline and bottom line.
4. In case both the entities were in the same activity and compete with each other, but after the M&A there will be one entity and therefore no mutual competition.

## Joint Venture:

When two companies join hands to form a joint venture to execute a particular type of business activity. This is temporary or restricted partnership, to complete the specific work or business activity. A joint venture is subject to the terms and conditions of a joint venture agreement. This kind joint venture can be formed between two Indian companies or between one Indian company and one foreign country.

Joint venture benefits both the promoters' companies. Some of the benefits are outlined here under.

1. **Eligibility in Acquiring the Contract** – Many time the companies do not fulfil the criteria to bid for various contract such as turnover, capital, experience etc. but when two companies form the joint venture, they will meet the criteria of bid and get the contract.

2. **Technology** – one company may be technology driven and therefore bring the technology required to execute work of specific venture and another company may have in depth knowledge of market and have competent manpower and experience to execute the work. If both the companies form the joint venture, they will successfully complete the work or specific contract.

3. **Area of Operation** - The joint venture can conduct the business in the operational areas of both the promoters' companies.

4. **Capital Contribution and Risk and Profit Sharing** – Both the promoters' companies will contribute the capital in joint venture which will enable them to take up capital intensive projects otherwise it might not have been possible by one promoter company. The promoter will share the risk and rewards as agreed between them, in the joint venture agreement.

To sum up, the entrepreneurs should make their all efforts to grow their enterprise in terms of sales and profit using all available opportunities.

•••

CHAPTER 17

# Package Designing and Packaging.

In the present era, packaging of products in properly designed packages is playing an important role in domestic and international business. Proper packaging is having following advantages.

1. Safety from any damage in transportation and handling.
2. Safety from climatic effect of different climatic zone.
3. Compliance with packaging criteria of different countries can be met.
4. Environmentally friendly and recyclable or biodegradable packaging material can be used as per rules of different countries.
5. Easy to handle the packaged product in entire logistic chain.
6. Packaging makes the product attractive, and the product can pack as per customer choice. This makes higher customer's satisfaction.

The following are some of the important points to be noted in the package design/selection of packaging.

1. **Product Specific Packaging:**

   Designing product specific package require a detail analysis from various angle like customer's choice and as per specification if any provided by customers, brand building, safety in transportation and handling in various logistic chain, Effect of climate change in different zone and the material should be environmentally friendly or biodegradable as per international norms and the country specific guidelines.

In the case of food and drug products, in addition to all the above criteria, the guidelines of food and drug controller and country specific norms should be followed. Idea of extra care in packaging of above products, is to protect their effectiveness, physical and chemical properties of all the ingredients such as colour, taste, aroma, and also to protect the products from dryness, moisture, light, temperature, chemical reactions, infective agents such as bacteria, fungi, parasites, and infestation agents such as insects and pests.

Entrepreneurs need to choose cost-effective packaging and modify it from time to time but of course keeping in view all the above criteria for domestic as well as international markets.

2. **Logistic And Distribution Specific Packaging:**

Design and packaging material and packaging method and size and dimension of packaging as per suitability of logistic and distribution chain is important aspect in the packaging. Bar code symbols are necessary on every packaging as per recent business trends. Likewise, brand name and logo [if it is finalized] need to be fixed on the packaging. The opinion of dealers/ distributors and customers if any should be kept in view regarding packaging. The following aspect will further add value to the packaging.

i. Quality of packing material.

ii. Description of material inside the package.

iii. Suitability for display of nutritional value in the case of food products.

iv. Suitability for display of contents in drug items

v. Suitability of display of Warning and precaution

vi. Suitability of display of bar code, price license, brand and logo.

vii. Marking for unpacking or unboxing on the packaging to avoid damage to the product.

3. **Convenience And Choice of Consumers:**

The consumers' choice or preference in packaging differs from person to person. We recommend that entrepreneurs take a broad outlook on graphics and design of packaging depending on the choice of majority of consumers and different market of their products. We mention hereunder some of the aspects of the packaging which are commonly preferred by the consumers.

i. Easy to carry, handle, open effortlessly or with opening devise provided with the products, close, empty, reuse, environment friendly and biodegradable etc.

ii. The cost of packaging should be reasonable so that the ultimate cost of the main product should not increase unreasonably.

iii. Packaging design should be appealing and attractive with brand and logo etc. when the products are displayed on consumer's shelves in the mall or supermarket or in retail store in comparison to the same products of competitors and as per market trend.

To sum up, we impress upon the entrepreneur to give utmost importance to package design and packaging of the products as per market trend and make it more appealing and attractive than the competitors to position the product high, for capturing maximum market share of same product range.

•••

CHAPTER 18

# Costing and Pricing are key Element of Profit

## Understand costing:

Entrepreneurs to understand correct calculation of production cost of their products and services to decides on sales price to make the profit.

The cost of the product should include the cost of raw materials, cost of consumables, proportionate depreciation, salary and wages of factory employees. Water and electricity, finance cost like interest and other charges, stationery and printing, cost of packaging, transportation cost of raw material up to the factory, rent if any, repair and maintenance and insurance cost will be cost of production and when the administrative cost like salary of administrative staff, traveling. Advertising and Marketing expenses, cost of after sales and service period etc. are added it will become the cost of sales of the product. The cost of sales as explained above or in other word total cost of product finally worked out is important to decide the selling price of the product while keeping the profit margin. It is worth understanding the direct and indirect types of cost at this juncture.

## Let's understand direct cost:

When the cost readily identified and which are directly related to produce the product is called as direct cost like cost of raw material, consumables, wages, and bonus paid to the labours, transportation of raw material to the factory, cost of any part directly purchased to assemble in the main product.

## Important precautions in the costing:

Entrepreneurs must carefully understand that the costing is the most crucial part of any business enterprise. It requires detailed studies of the production process and intricacies with regards to sales. There are many items of expenses or cost which might have been missed out while calculating the total cost of products. We give here under the cost which needs careful consideration.

1] Wastage of material during the production process.

2] Rejection of products does not confer to quality test, or some defects are noticed after production of the product.

3] Rejection, return and replacement of the products by the customers.

4] Sale on the credit which blocks the funds and leads to finance cost. The realization of some percentage of credit sales may be delayed or may not be recovered at all. Hence it all costs the company or enterprise and for those necessary provisions to be made.

5] Payment of GST or any other taxes, by the enterprise while purchasing the raw material, but the input credit will be received when the product is sold. This will lead to finance cost to the enterprise.

To sum up, it is impressed upon the entrepreneurs to undertake the costing exercise and find ways to reduce the cost of products carefully. Once the final cost of products has arrived, then decides the selling cost after keeping the profit margin. They should also study the pattern of the sales price and quality of products of competitors so that they can keep the sales price competitive for their products to capture a good market share.

•••

CHAPTER 19

# Maintain High Quality Standards

"Customers pay only for what is of use to them and this gives them value. Nothing else constitutes value" – Peter Drucker

In the prevailing economic situation, new approaches are called for. Companies are adopting a new system of technology and management for both internal and external purposes. The use of total quality Management [TQM] system for developing, manufacturing and supplying the required products and services meeting customer expectations and satisfaction becoming more important for success of an entrepreneur.

Quality management has thus become a most important management function. Entrepreneurs need to take the appropriate actions to identify and understand customer's needs and ensure that the same are met through quality products and services. Market trend shows that quality, cost effectiveness and time bound delivery are important points for the entrepreneurs to register success in domestic and export markets.

Progress of both domestic as well as export-oriented enterprises are very necessary for economic development of the country and to achieve the good growth in sales turnover of these enterprises the quality products and services which meets customers' needs are imperative. Export is vital for economic development thereby foreign currency is received in the country which will be utilized for payments of imports and surplus is kept for future requirement. Therefore, it's more important for

Export oriented enterprises to maintain the quality of products and services because inferior quality can damage the reputation and image of the exporter entrepreneur and of the exporting country in the eyes of importer and importer country.

We quote hereunder what" W.Edward Deming" in his book "OUT OF CRISES" says about customers.

1] "Dissatisfied customers does not complain: he switches."

2] "It will not suffice to have Customer that are merely satisfied. Customers that are unhappy and some that are merely satisfied switch. Profit comes from repeat customers - those that boast about the product or service." -

This is also true that once the customer switches to another seller he may not come back to you in normal course of business easily.

In this context, we impress upon the entrepreneurs to maintain the quality of your products and services up to the satisfaction of your domestic as well as overseas customers to be a successful entrepreneur.

## Quality is a key to success:

Quality denotes all the specialties of the products and services that make them superior and excellent in comparison to products and services available on the market front. Another aspect is the products and services should be made available consistently of superior quality at competitive, affordable prices and delivered within the time frame agreed time schedule. It's important that products and services should be upgraded from time to time in accordance with demand in the market and post-sales services should be an integral part of sales of products and services. We may conclude that quality is the imperative part of business management. Monitoring the performance of products/ services provided and taking corrective steps if any week link or deficiency noticed is imperative to be a market leader. The entrepreneur should also focus on customers feedback, reviews, and customer's satisfaction, because ultimately business will come from highly satisfied customers only which will generate the profit for the enterprise.

To sum up, successful entrepreneurs always focus on the quality of their products and services and ensure that they are the best out of the best at competitive prices, coupled with excellent post-sales services which lead to high customer's satisfaction.

•••

CHAPTER 20

# Risk Assessment and Risk Mitigation:

A risk is an unavoidable event that may affect any business enterprises, specialty when the circumstances are beyond the control of the entrepreneurs. The risk can be classified in to three categories -

**1] External Risk such as-**

a] **Natural calamities** - like floods, drought, earthquakes, pandemics, Fire etc.

**Mitigation** - Entrepreneurs should cover such risk in the insurance policy. The disaster management team handles the situation to minimize the loss and restart the business operation.

b] **Man made disturbances** - like riots, violence, labour strikes.

**Mitigation** - Insurance coverage and if labour strikes is related to workers of own enterprise the efforts should be made to negotiate with them and resolve their grievances. Such conditions should be handled by the disaster management team.

c] **Change in govt law or policy and put ban on the product.**

**Mitigation** - The entrepreneurs should keep themselves with the business news and when they get any clue of change in the policy, they should immediately go for diversification to other products which can be possible with minor changes in the unit. If diversification is not possible, the entrepreneurs should go for any new activity and new products and try to use old assets in new business activity, and the assets not of any use may be disposed- off quickly. The timely recognition of risk and taking appropriate steps quickly to minimize the risk.

d] **Market risk -**

This kind of risk arises due to volatility of the market such as high inflation rate when the situation becomes such that the people may not have the buying capacity beyond their essential daily needs. Other reasons may be price fluctuations, new and advance products launched in the market by competitors, Market trend is changed, Customers preference, choices are changed.

**Mitigation** - Make the product as per market trend and customers choice. Obtain customer feedback regularly to know their choices. Reduce the cost of production to reduce the market price to meet the competition. Establish the positioning of your product by brand building so that people remain attached with the products. Give better after-sales service than your competitors. Introduce some combo packs and coupons, to increase the sales. Also find out new market for your products and resort to deep penetration in existing territory.

e] **Operational risk** - This risk is due to breakdown of plant and machinery, electricity failure or short circuits, Technology become old and new technology or upgradation not yet done, failure of computer system, Information technology, cyber security breach, and hacking of accounts and data, virus attack, death or serious illness of key personals etc.

**Prevention of risk** – The entrepreneur should be vigilant to recognize the potential risk or threat, and accordingly he should take the necessary proactive steps to prevent such risk. Like virus attack in computer systems, the antivirus can be installed. Taking back up on a regular basis will also be a preventive measure against loss of the data. Entrepreneurs should always make necessary changes to upgrade the technology to the latest technology so that they can prevent the risk associated with old technology like higher cost of production and lower quality of product and less output.

**Mitigation of risk** – Whatever operational risk can be covered in insurance policy; the entrepreneurs must cover the same. Further the disaster management team should be kept ready always to handle the situation. Second line of defence should be built to continue the operation in case of death or serious illness of key personals. Efforts should be made to restore and continue the business as per the business continuity plan in place.

Apart from the above the following risk should also be considered important:

## 1. Sales risk and its mitigation:

The risk of rapid sales decline is one of the most critical risks. It depends on fixed and variable costs. The selling risk is very high due to fixed costs and the break-even point may be too close to the sale price. A slight drop in sales is a result of the sale of products below the break-even point. Therefore, it is important to lower the break-even point. This can be done by reducing fixed costs wherever possible and converting fixed costs into variable costs. In the early stages of the business, the fixed costs should be kept on the lower side or minimum to the extent possible and the product cost per unit also needs to be kept to the minimum possible level. In order to reduce the sales risk, fixed and variable costs should be balanced, and the balance of fixed and variable costs should be calculated properly. Another way to reduce the sales risk is to go for diversification after a proper study of the cost of production of the products, their sale price, and the margin of profit available on such products.

### 2. Cash flow risk and risk mitigation:

Cash flow risk is the risk when an entrepreneur needs cash quickly. The cash flow risk arises mainly when bills are not realized in time due to a delay in dispatch or the receivable has not been released on time. Such risk is to be mitigated by way of an uninterrupted production process and timely dispatch of the products and timely realization of receivables by making all-out efforts.

### 3. Production risk and risk mitigation:

Any interruption or bottleneck in production is considered as a production risk. The unit's greatest production risk is power shortages. The entrepreneurs can consider installing the generator of the required capacity to reduce production loss due to power shortages. Sudden malfunctions of machines and systems can create production risks. It is therefore necessary, that the equipment and plant and machinery should be covered under an annual maintenance contract after the warranty period is expired.

### 4. Social risk and risk mitigation:

Such risk by nature may crop up sometime when society starts taking objection regarding products or its process in particular regions due to their religious belief or some social leader has influenced the mindset of the society. Such a risk can be mitigated by explaining the facts about the product and the process of production. The advertisement to remove doubt in the mind can be given in press media and on television.

To sum up, entrepreneurs should recognize the potential risk and take preventive measures and plan for mitigation of risk if the prevention of threat or risk is not possible.

•••

CHAPTER 21

# Banking - Basic Knowledge

Entrepreneurs should have a basic knowledge of Banking as they will be required to deal with banks daily. There may be an occasion to raise the funds from Banks.

1. **Banking structure -** The Banking structure in the country comprises with one central Bank of the country known as Reserve Bank of India who regulate the banking system and public sector banks namely State bank of India and Nationalized. banks, Cooperative banks, Private Sector banks, Regional Rural Banks, Payment banks Small Finance Banks and Non-Banking Financial companies.

2. **Function of Banks –** Banks' core activity is raising funds by way of accepting the deposits and providing need-based fund and non-fund facilities to the customers. Transfer of funds, selling of mutual funds, insurance, credit cards are some of the other activities being undertaken by most of the Banks.

We discuss the important aspects of banking hereunder.

**1. Types of Deposit Accounts:** The Banks open various types of deposit accounts like Saving Bank account, Current account, and fixed deposit accounts.

**i. Saving Bank account** – Any individual single or jointly with other individuals can open a Saving Bank account. Bank allows personal transactions in these accounts. Salary accounts of employees and pension accounts are mostly saving bank accounts. Business entities are not entitled to open saving bank accounts for their business transaction. All facilities like cheque book facility, Online banking, Mobile banking, Debit cards, IMPS/ NEFT/ RTGS, UPI Payments are available to the account holder. Bank pays some nominal interest in Saving account to its customers. The facility of auto transfer from saving bank account to Fixed deposit account is also available keeping certain minimum balance in saving bank account and when the funds are required, it will be retransferred from fixed deposit account to saving bank account. One can transact up to a maximum number of transactions in your saving bank account as per category of your account which depends on the average balance maintained by the account holder in his account.

**ii. Current account** - current account can be opened by individuals singly or jointly as well as the business firms/ companies for their business transactions. Banks have some charges for maintaining current accounts. In current accounts facilities of cheque book, online transactions, IMPS/ NEFT/ RTGS, UPI Payments, Debit card is available to the customers.

**iii. Fixed deposit accounts** - Fixed deposit accounts can be opened by any individual singly or jointly or firms or company or any other legally constituted entities. Funds are deposited for a fixed period in such accounts and banks pay the compounding interest on the deposit. The depositors will have options to withdraw the interest on monthly/quarterly/half yearly / yearly basis or at the time of maturity.

All the above can be opened after submission of proof of your photo identity such as PAN card and address proof driving license/Aadhar card / passport etc., which is commonly known as KYC [know your customer] documents. Verification of customers will be done based on Face to Face or by video system.

**2. Types of Credit Facilities:** Banks provide various types of credit facilities categorized in different categories depending on purpose, nature of facilities, tenure of facility. The entrepreneurs should be aware of such Credit facilities available from the banking sector so that they can approach the banks when the need arises. The following types of credit facilities classified as per nature of credit facilities are available for business enterprises:

i. **Term loan Facility**- The term loan facility is available to finance the fixed assets or capital assets like, land and building, plant and machinery, furniture, and fixtures etc. The term loan is repayable in instalments over a period which depends on estimation of profit generated by the unit based on which repayment capacity is to be worked out and useful life of assets created out of bank loan. Generally, the total tenor of loan in majority cases ranges from 5 years to 9 years and for infrastructure projects it goes up to 15 years. The loan instalments commenced usually after the commercial operation date i.e., when commercial products start.

ii. **Overdraft Facility**- Overdraft facilities generally provided by the banks to the customers occasionally having satisfactory track record for short period for meeting urgent working capital expenses.

iii. **Demand Loan** - Demand loans are those which are repayable on demand. These are also for the short term and for the total tenor of not exceeding 36 months.

iv. **Cash Credit [CC] facility**- This is commonly granted by the banks to the enterprises for meeting their working capital. The bank assesses the working capital limit required for one operating cycle from purchase of raw material to realization of sales proceeds. After the limit is fixed you can avail the limit for purchase of raw material for your enterprise and you will be required to submit your stock and debtor position every month and based on which bank will decide your drawing power after deduction of margin fixed by the bank. The facility shall be renewed every year. If your business is increased your cc limit shall also increase subject to satisfactory conduct of your account and if your business is decreased the cc limit may be decreased by your bank.

v. **Pre shipment and Post Shipment Credit** – These credit facilities are related to export activities. Pre shipment credit means the credit facility required to purchase the raw material to make the finished product and post shipment credit facility means, when the goods are exported and invoice are raised, but payment will be received after goods are reached to destination, so bank will provide the finance against export bills till the payment from overseas buyers received.

vi. **Bank guarantee** – Bank guarantee is a non-fund credit facility. When one entity [ say party A] give some order to execute the specific work, to another entity [ say party B], but party A wants from party B, the Bank guarantee so that if the party B fails in completion of work as per quality and within time, the party A will get the bank guarantee amount from the bank to recover the loss if happened due to delayed completion or non-completion of work by party B. The payment of bank guarantee amount made by bank to party A is called invocation of bank guarantee and Bank will recover this amount from party B immediately. Bank guarantees are usually required by contractors to secure the contracts relating to infrastructure sectors from governments or their agencies.

vii. **Letter of Credits** – This is a non-fund-based facility, and it is required for sale and purchase of goods. When the seller supplies the goods to buyer, he will require the payment from the buyer, but buyer cannot pay the seller immediately, in this situation buyer approach his bank to issue letter of credit in favour of seller, so that seller can get the payment from bank for the supplies made by him. LC issuing bank when make the payment under

Letter of credit, in turn he recovers the same from the buyer along with interest, cost and charges relating to the above transaction.

viii. **Types of loan/credit facilities as per purpose and category of borrowers** - Banks provide the loans/ credit facility depending on repayment capacity of the borrower and in some cases, it also considers the value of security along with repayment capacity of borrowers. Some of example of such loans are given hereunder-

a. Personal loan for any personal needs like education, medical needs.

b. Home loan for purchase house/flat/ plot and construction thereon/ repair and renovation of old house.

c. Loan against property for any personal or business needs

d. Vehicle loans for purchase of commercial vehicles or personal vehicles.

e. Education loan for pursuing degree/diploma or other education programs in India or abroad.

f. Loan to traders and medium small and micro enterprises. This is for establishing a business or its expansion.

g. Corporate credit to big companies. This is for big companies in sole banking/multiple banking or consortium finance.

In the above category 1 to 5 are self-explanatory as per the purpose and category 6-7 are mainly for business purpose as discussed in detail above in this chapter.

**3. Ancillary Banking Services:** Remittances by way of Demand Drafts, RTGS, NEFT E banking, Mobile Banking, credit cards, mutual funds, and insurance under tie up arrangements etc.

**4. Dealing with the bank:** It is very important for running the enterprise successfully that the entrepreneur should establish a satisfactory track record of dealing with the banks. They should take care that their cheques or electronic fund transfer mandates do not bounce back. Repayment of loan instalments/interest is made strictly on time. All the sales and purchases should be routed through the bank account and whatever monthly/quarterly/half yearly/yearly statement stipulated by the bank should be submitted on time. This all will contribute to your better credit score and hold your hand and all ups and downs of your business enterprise. It is important for the entrepreneur that the major cost of running a business is the Finance Cost, therefore the funds availed from the bank should be judicially used only for the purpose the funds are availed. In other words, the end use of the banks funds if verified by the bank should be proved by documentary evidence at the time of the physical verification of capital assets purchased out of bank loan and value of stock inventory, debtors etc. created with bank working capital facility. An entrepreneur is expected to manage the working capital effectively by proper inventory management by giving timely order and for required quantity at well negotiated price, Debtors Management by ensuring recovery of credit sales within the time period, creditors management by making timely payment of supplies and cash management by depositing cash received during the course of business, to minimize the finance cost.

To sum up, entrepreneurs can take the required support from their banker by maintaining satisfactory conduct of their loan/credit facilities accounts.

•••

CHAPTER 22

# Purchasing of Capital Assets and Raw Material - A Proper Approach:

Entrepreneurs must take due care of rates. Quality, brands, market reputation of supplier while purchasing capital assets as well as the raw material. We discuss hereunder some of the important points for the benefit of entrepreneurs.

**Purchasing of capital assets -**

1] **Purchase of industrial land and building/shed** - The entrepreneurs should consider location, topography, availability of water, electricity, sewage lines, connecting roads, constructed area etc. while purchasing the industrial land and building/shed. They should get the title of the property verified by legal experts to ensure that the property is having clear title and is free from any encumbrances. It is always preferred to purchase such property in an industrial area for industries/ or commercial or Information technology park depending on nature of your business where all the facilities required for the business are available. The price of the property should be negotiated and finalized as per the prevailing market rate or lower than that price.

2] **Purchasing of plant and machinery/equipment/ accessories [ P&M]-**

i] Finalize the latest technology based on which your enterprise is to work carefully considering the cost of various available options.

ii] Select the P&M and study their specification and cost and compare such specification and cost with other manufacturers/suppliers. Short list the manufacturers/supplier.

iii] Negotiate the cost with shortlisted manufacturers/ suppliers and finalize the manufacturer /supplier [vendor] whose brand is well established and is ready to supply at the lowest rate and provide aftersales service and give the warranty of their products. Take advantage of market competition.

iv] Better to get the credentials of vendor verified from some reliable sources/ their websites or local enquiry. If the credentials are good and vendor is reputed then place the order mentioning specification of P&M, to be purchased. Advance payment that too whatever minimum possible to be made only in cases of branded products manufactured by reputed companies and supplied by reputed authorized dealers.

Entrepreneurs should keep a proper record of all the capital assets purchased for their knowledge and ready reference / information as and when needed.

## Purchase of raw material -

Raw material and consumables are required to be purchased by every enterprise on a regular basis, however raw material contributes a major part between the two. The local suppliers who can supply the raw material of the required quality should be preferred over an outside supplier. Entrepreneurs may work out the quantity for each lot to be purchased based on yearly requirement. Deciding of quantity per lot is important because it carries the transportation cost and price difference on purchase of minimum quantity.

Calculation of the required raw-material stock according to availability of the same. The above principle should be followed in purchasing of consumables also. The rates for raw materials and consumables should be negotiated properly, taking advantage of market competition.

The raw material and consumable purchased should be recorded every time and whenever they are taken out for further processing should also be recorded. This will facilitate knowing the available stock of raw materials and consumables at any given point of time.

To sum up, purchasing fixed assets and raw materials at a reasonable price makes the good beginning of the entrepreneurial journey.

●●●

CHAPTER 23

# Working Capital Management

Efficient and productive use of all long-term and short-term funds is the essence of financial management. In other words, the success of any enterprise depends on proper use of capital infused by the promoter as well as funds raised from various sources in the form of unsecured loans, secured loans, short term loan and working limits. Means all the items of liabilities side of balance sheet called as sources of funds and the same should be used for the purpose it has been raised for built up of fixed assets and current assets which is termed as uses of funds. Diversion of funds may heavily cost the entrepreneur. To understand working capital management better, lets understand the management of long-term funds together with working capital management as explained hereunder:

## 1] Management of long-term funds -

Long term funds are used for the creation of fixed immovable or movable assets or other capital assets. It aims to use long term funds judiciously when purchasing fixed assets such as factory's land building, plant and machinery, equipment, furniture, and fixture etc. Funds for creation of fixed assets or capital assets should always come from long term sources and never use the short-term funds for creation of fixed assets or capital assets, otherwise it will lead to shortage of working capital to run the business successfully. It is vital aspect for the enterprise that after meeting the long-term fund requirement for purchase of fixed assets, the balance amount of long-term funds shall form the margin of safety and it is also called net working capital.

## 2] Working capital management –

Working capital management is most crucial to running the business. The total or gross working capital is the sum of current assets, while net working capital is the excess of current assets over current liabilities. In other words, net working capital is the portion of working capital that is funded from long-term sources and determines the margin of safety for meeting current liabilities.

Working capital management is important for the following reasons:

a) Working capital facility if availed from bank bears the interest costs, hence its judicial use is necessary to minimize the interest burden.

b) Fixed assets are acquired occasionally, and financial decisions are required only occasionally. However, working capital management requires ongoing decisions and the same often requires significant financial resources.

c) In an inflationary situation where commodity prices are constantly on the rise, if working capital is not managed efficiently, there may not be enough money to buy commodities at the right time and production will be hampered.

The goal of efficient working capital management is to ensure smooth operation of the working capital cycle which comprises of cash - purchase of raw material - manufacturing of finished product - cash sales - and then - cash. When there are credit sales, this cycle will be extended for the period by which the value of credit sales is realized.

The working capital turnover ratio is an important tool to monitor how many times working capital gets rotated in a year in relation to net sales. It is calculated as - Net sales divided by working capital. [ Here working capital is equal to Current assets- current liabilities]. Here it is worthwhile to mention the working capital ratio which is calculated as - current assets divided by current liabilities. This is also called current ratio or liquidity ratio. If this ratio is 1.33:1 it depicts that the current assets are sufficient to meet the current liabilities of the enterprise.

The company should maintain sufficient cash to cover the day-to-day costs of production, sales, and other operations, while ensuring that the company maintains adequate inventory levels. Holding excess inventory means blocking of funds which carries higher costs in the form of interest, and it ultimately results in lower profitability. Therefore, companies must accurately assess their working capital needs for maintaining adequate inventory and other current assets.

## Concept of the Operating cycle:

Fundamental to determining a company's working capital requirements is the concept of the operating cycle. The operating cycle is the cycle in which goods are purchased using cash. Raw materials are converted into work-in-progress and finished goods. Finished goods are sold to customers in cash or on credit. When sales happen on credit, the cash is blocked in the form of receivable. Once the receivables are realized, the funds are cycled back into cash and can be used to purchase goods such as raw material, consumables etc. and this cycle shall continue. The working capital used by a company at any point of time will be the sum of the following values:

a) cash and bank balances.

b) value of raw material and consumable at cost price.

c) value of work-in-progress at cost of production.

d) value of finished goods at cost of sales.

e) an amount of receivables or sundry debtors.

An entrepreneur or his/her finance officer should work out the working capital requirement based on holding period of inventory and other current assets and after due consideration of credit available from supplier.

## Cash and bank balance:

The amount of cash and bank balance. a business should hold depends on the following factors:

a) **Trading volume:**

   The cash and bank balance depend on sales volume if the sales is mostly in cash. However, a balance must be struck between cash inflows from sales and cash outflows from day-to-day purchase and operating expenses. The entrepreneur should maintain minimum cash in hand and rest amount of cash they should deposit in the bank only. If the entrepreneur is enjoying cash credit facility from bank, the surplus cash should be deposited in their cash credit account to minimize the interest burden.

b) **Urgent needs:**

   Entrepreneur should keep a certain amount of cash in hand or in their bank account in reserve for unforeseen circumstances.

c] **Cash flow fluctuations:**

   Enterprise should keep different cash balances at different stages of the month, consistent with their monthly cash flow forecast.

## Funds required for raw material:

The funds required for raw material depends on the following factors:

1] **Holding period** - Holding is calculated in relation to yearly raw material consumption. For example, yearly consumption of raw material is INR 24 Lakhs and raw material equivalent to one month consumption is required to be purchased in every lot, that means holding period is one month and amount of raw material is INR 2 Lakhs.

2) **Lead period in days** - Lead period in days is the time lag between placing an order and receiving the actual material. If payment is made in advance while placing the order, the same is to be shown in advance payment in current assets.

3) **Minimum Order Quantity** – Many suppliers fixed minimum order quantity of the materials to be supplied by them, hence while calculating the raw material holding period and amount required for that, should be kept in view, to purchase the raw material from the supplier.

4] **Other important factors of purchase of raw materials-**

   i. Transportation/shipping costs- This is the important cost factor as it directly relates to the quantity of raw material to be purchased. For example, the capacity of the truck is 12 MT and if the purchase quantity of raw material is 8 MT, the transport company will charge approximately the same transportation charges as applicable for 12MT raw material. Accordingly, entrepreneurs to decide the quantity of raw material to be purchased keeping in view the transportation charges to be incurred.

   ii. Storage and insurance cost – Entrepreneurs should decide the quantity of raw material such that they should not incur the avoidable cost on storage. At the same time insurance premiums will be higher if the stock of raw material is higher.

## Funds required for stock in process:

The holding period and amount of stock in process is calculated in terms of cost of production and is mainly depends on the completion time of the manufacturing process. The longer the manufacturing process, the higher the investment in stock in process and vice versa. Stock in process is also high when the manufacturing process requires the use of multiple machines, and the capacities of these machines are below the required capacity.

## Finished product:

The holding period amount of finished goods is calculated in relation to cost of sales and determined by the following factors:

a) Expected quantity of sales.

b) Time required for inspection of goods

d) If the customer requires delivery in big lots, more finished goods should be maintained.

e) If the optimal production quantity is large, the quantity of finished goods will also be large.

The stock of raw materials, stock in process and finished goods combinedly terms as inventory. Here it's important to understand inventory turnover over ratio which is calculated as- Cost of goods sold divided by average inventory. The ratio can be also calculated as- Net sales divided by Average inventory at cost or as – Net sales divided by average inventory at selling price. This ratio gives an idea that how many times the inventory is rotated in a year.

## Funds required for sundry debtors or receivables:

The holding period and amount of receivable is calculated on amount net credit sales and depends on the customer's payment terms agreed between the buyer and seller. Many times, discount is given if the payment is made immediately after delivery, Entrepreneurs to note that credit sales should be done with caution to good customers only otherwise some customers may not pay the amount in time, or they may not pay at all, and this may result into loss to your company. It is advisable that entrepreneur should make vigorous follow up from their debtors [if they did not pay their dues on date] to get funds realized from them as soon as possible and next time they should not supply the goods to such person who has not repaid their dues on time.

The Debtors' turnover ratio is calculated as - net credit sales divided by average receivables, which gives a fair idea about the movement of receivables in relation to net credit sales.

Sundry creditors or account payable – The enterprise purchases the raw material from their supplier who provides credit on supplies made by them and on the due date buyer has to make the payment to the supplier. This credit supply may be without interest or with interest as per the mutually agreed terms and conditions between the buyer and seller. The creditors turn ratio gives an idea that how many times the purchase is available on credit in relation to total credit purchase and the ratio is calculated as – Total credit purchase divided by average sundry creditor.

## Working capital resource planning:

The main recourse for the entrepreneurs is to obtain a working capital limit which is commonly known as cash credit limit from a commercial bank. This is easy as the commercial banks are also looking for an opportunity to lend the funds. Bank shall increase the limit if there is increase in the business and decrease the same when there is down word trend in the business. The entrepreneurs should keep their conduct of account satisfactory for availing the maximum facilities from the bank. The banks calculate the working capital normally as under –

**1] Method - A**

A] Total current assets =

B] Less current liabilities other than bank borrowing =

C] Working capital gap [A-B] =

D] Less 25% margin or net working capital [whichever is higher] =

E] Maximum permissible bank finance [ C-D] =

The figures arrived in E above is working capital limit or cash credit limit to be considered for working capital requirement of the unit.

**2] Method -B**

The banks for MSME sector, if they require a limit of up INR 5 crores calculate the eligible working capital limit @ of 20% of sales turnover. That means if the sales turnover is INR 25 Crores, they shall consider the limit up to INR 5 Crores.

However out of above two methods the maximum limit worked out in any of the above methods shall be considered for proposals up to INR 5 Crores but for proposals of above INR 5 Crore only limit work out by method - A above shall be considered.

To sum up, entrepreneurs should ensure financial management professionally to make maximum utilization of funds prudently to run the business and make the profit.

●●●

CHAPTER 24

# Break-Even Analysis

The break-even analysis is a method to know what is the minimum production level at which the cost incurred to produce the products is equal to the sale amount. That means at this point you can meet all the costs without incurring loss or profit and this point is known as the breakeven point. To earn a reasonable profit, an entrepreneur have to plan to increase production above the level of breakeven point. Breakeven point is important for entrepreneur to maintain the production level of his enterprise, and it is also important for the lenders who lend the money to establish the enterprise to judge the profitability of the enterprise.

## 1. Understand Break even Analysis:

To conduct profit-oriented business activity, certain costs are involved such as raw material cost, salaries/wages, interest charges on borrowed funds and the capital cost invested in the business activity, and all these costs put together termed as the total cost.

The total cost comprises of two types of cost as follows-

(i) Fixed Cost and

(ii) Variable Cost.

### Fixed Cost:

Fixed Cost is that cost which remains constant irrespective of the production level. such as, interest cost on term loan, rent of factory/office if on rent, depreciation on fixed assets, municipal taxes etc. These costs are to be incurred irrespective of whether the factory is working at all or closed or its working on full capacity or partial capacity. These costs or termed as fixed costs.

For example, a factory rent is INR10000/- and interest on borrowed term loan is INR5000/ per month and it produces 150 units of product per month, assuming that except above there is no other cost is involved, the fixed cost per unit in this case comes to INR100/-. In case production increases next month to 300 unit, in that case fixed cost per unit decreased to INR50/- and if production decrease to 100 unit, the per unit fixed cost increase to INR150/- That means fixed cost remain the same irrespective of number of units produced and per unit fixed cost is inversely proportionate to number of units produced in a particular month means if no of units produced more the fixed cost per unit decrease and if number of units produced less the fixed cost per unit increase.

## Variable Costs:

Variable Cost is increase or decrease with the increase in production or decrease in production, respectively. It is directly proportionate to the number of units produced. For example, raw material consumed is directly related to the number of units produced. The variable cost remains the same for every unit produced. It can be further elaborated as under –

If Raw-material cost per unit is INR 100/- then to produce 10 units, the raw material cost will be INR1000/-.

Variable Cost per unit = Rs.100/-

Once the concept of fixed cost and variable cost is clear, we can easily calculate the Breakeven point.

## Calculation of the Breakeven point:

Before calculating the Breakeven point, we must calculate the contribution. The contribution is the difference between the variable cost per unit and selling price per unit is the contribution. The contribution remains the same if there is no change in the variable cost per unit and selling price per unit. Hence, given the same selling price, the difference between Variable Cost per unit and selling price per unit which we call 'Contribution' also remains the same. The total Contribution increases when sales of total number of units increases. If the fixed cost remains the same, and the enterprise sells such number of units by that the contribution becomes equal to the Fixed Cost, such number of unit or the sales receipts is called the breakeven point. At this point there no profit and no loss. Any contribution made above the breakeven point or say after meeting the fixed cost, shall be the Profit for the enterprise.

We can summarize the above conclusion as under:

i). Total Cost of production [COP] = Variable Cost multiply by No. of units (VC) + Fixed Cost.

ii). Contribution (C) = Sales Receipt (SR) – Variable Cost (VC)

iii). Profit (P) at "N" level of production =

(Sales Receipt for "N" No. of Units) – Total Cost. Or

SR – (VC + FC) or SR – VC – FC

Profit = Contribution (SR-VC) – Fixed Cost (FC)

| | | |
|---|---|---|
| Selling Price per unit | - | INR 100.00 |
| Variable Cost per unit | - | INR 50.00 |
| Fixed Cost for the Project | - | INR.1.00 LAKH |
| Production Levels: | | 5000 units |
| Sales Receipt | | INR 5.00LAKH |
| Variable Cost | | INR 2.50 LAKH |
| Contribution | | INR 2.50 LAKH |
| Net profit [contribution- fixed cost] = | | INR 1.50 LAKH |

In the above if the number of units produced were 2000, the sales receipt was INR 2.00Lakhs, VC INR 1.00 Lakhs contribution comes to INR 1.00 Lakhs and fixed cost is 1.00 Lakh which is equal to contribution. Thus, this is the breakeven point in terms of production of the number of units and sales price.

**i] Break even in terms of Capacity Utilization:**

Break - Even level of production can be calculated using the below noted formula -

$$\text{BEP-} = \frac{\text{Fixed cost}}{\text{SR} - \text{VC} \quad \text{x total capacity}} \text{ x \%}$$

**ii] break even in terms of Sales Receipts:**

Break - Even Point in terms of Sales Receipts is calculated by fixed Cost and 'Profit Volume Ratio which is in short called P/V ratio. The importance of p/v ratio is that it depicts the relation between 'Contribution' (Sales Receipt - Variable Cost) and Sales. In other words, it is the percentage of Contribution to the sales volume. It that what percentage of sales receipt will be available after setting off the variable cost, to meet fixed cost and book the profit.

P/V Ratio = Contribution/Sales = SR - VC/SR

If contribution is 5000 and sales receipt will be 10000, the PV ratio will be 0.5 or 50 % of sales receipt to meet the fixed cost and book the profit.

We can calculate Breakeven Sales Receipt with following Formula:

Fixed cost/PV ratio or $\frac{\text{Fixed cost}}{\text{SR-VC /SR}}$

## Importance of Break - Even Analysis:

The break-even analysis is very important to judge the financial viability of any project, some of the important benefits are as under-.

1) It is a helpful tool for entrepreneurs to choose the activity, for investors to make the investment decision and bankers or lenders for making credit decision.
2) It helps the entrepreneur to know the sensitivity to price or sales fluctuations on profitability.
3) Entrepreneurs producing or planning to produce multiple products can compare the BEP for each product and concentrate on more profitable products.
4) In the event of heavy price fluctuations, it helps the entrepreneurs to change the products OR process to do the business above the BEP to make the profit.
5) Breakeven analysis helps the entrepreneur in product pricing. The entrepreneur may plan for allowing discount on the product to the extent if BEP is within the comfortable range after discount.

To sum up, entrepreneurs should make the best use of break-even analysis to make a proper decision of going for a particular product and decide the pricing so that their enterprise earns a sufficient profit.

•••

CHAPTER 25

# Time Tested Marketing and Sales Strategy

When entrepreneurs think about starting their entrepreneurial journey, they select the product only after studying its position of the demand and supply in the market. Many times, the product is considered suitable looking to its heavy demand of that product in the market and some time looking to success of some enterprises working in that product or in consideration of short supply of a particular product in the market whereas the product is having good demand. Marketing consists of various important activities.

## 1. Market survey or Market Research:

Market survey or market research is the first step to ascertain the demand and supply of the product for selection of product. After selection of product proper techno economic study should be carried out to study whether to set up a manufacturing unit of the selected product is a viable proposition. Here consumers' choice and their satisfaction are of prime importance. Entrepreneurs should continue their market research even after launching their product as this helps them to upgrade or modify their product and or packaging from time to time as per satisfaction of their customers.

## 2. Strategic Planning:

Planning for the marketing of the product get started with the start of the project and it should continue as an ongoing process at every stage of the project. Planning should cover setting up of distribution channels, digital and social media marketing, Market development advertisements, online sale on ecommerce platform, designing and packaging, logistic and supply chain arrangement, exploring new territory and deeper market penetration, estimation of future sales and sales promotion strategies.

## 3. Product Branding and logo:

The branding and logo of the product is necessary to position the product in the market and earn the trust of the customers. The customer treats the unbranded products of poor quality. This is a fact that there are several products of a similar type but of a different quality available in the market. Because of this reason the customers do not get the confidence and go for purchase of the unbranded product. Therefore, brand building is utmost necessary. Apart from building trust of the customers, it helps the customers and retailers in easy identification of the product, display of product on retailers show room and, in the mall, increase the brand image of the product and it will attract the customers to buy the product. Once the brand is established, the loyal customers will demand the products by brand only. Brand with logo on the products and packaging will further improve the visibility of the products, which will increase the faith of the customers and will result in to increase of the sale of the products.

## 4. Pricing of the product:

The price is a sensitive issue for the customers when they choose to buy the product more often, particularly when the quality of the product is the same as other competitors.

Keeping the above customers behaviour in mind, the pricing of the product should be done as under

1. keep the price based on profit margin at different levels of sales in a business cycle subject to condition that it should not be much higher than the similar products available in the market.
2. Price should be attractive for the customers subject to condition that it should be above the cost price so that it generates some profit. Customers purchase the products only when pricing is competitive with other market players.
3. Price may be kept slightly above the cost price to earn marginal profit only if there is some campaign for limited period to develop the market and once the customer's liking is developed price may be increased to earn the reasonable profit. Another way is to give some discount keeping the standard price intact or give some gift item as a combo pack keeping a combine price at such level that it gives some marginal profit.

## 5. Robust product Distribution system:

The aim of a robust distribution channel is to deliver the goods to the maximum consumers in the desired quantity within the prescribed time. To facilitate that the product should reach the customers when they need it most, and this can be achieved by creating a good network of distributors, dealers, whole sellers, retailers, sales outlets and vendors. Ecommerce platforms can be used for the sale of products and prompt delivery to the customers. Entrepreneurs may avail themselves of the services of the fastest couriers to deliver the product at the doorstep of the buyers within the shortest time.

## 6. Selling of the product to the customers:

The selling of the product is simply the delivery of the goods to the customers and recovering the price from them. Sales remain incomplete if the price of the goods sold to the customers is unrecovered. If the selling is by sales staff working on a salary basis or on a commission basis, by contacting the customers in person, in such a situation the sales staff should be well versed in product quality and specifications to get the best results.

The sales staff should be highly motivated and those who bring the best results should be rewarded with some incentives or appreciation or both.

It is also very important to supervise and monitor the sales staff at regular intervals by taking their meetings and through statements and returns.

If an outside agency is appointed for sale, in that case the agency who has done well should be rewarded with some gifts or with some bulk discount on selling goods above the sales targets.

## 7. Facility of after sales services:

This is an essential part of selling the products to the customers and it is more important if the product is of a technical nature. The entrepreneur must make an enquiry on the customer's complaint and resolve the complaint quickly and amicably, so that the customer is satisfied with the services of the enterprise. get impressed and become a repeat customer if he gets the satisfactory after sales services. The satisfied customers always spread positive news for the product and the enterprise, which will ultimately boost the sales of the company.

## 8. Sales Promotion and advertising:

This sales promotion activity in today's time is an ongoing process, to boost up the sales, particularly at the time of festivals or for the purpose of stock clearance. The sale promotion is resorted to sale the slow-moving item with the fast-moving item. Many enterprises give special discounts during the sales promotion campaign organized for a few days. Sometime special contest for particular period is arranged and winners are rewarded.

If you give advertisements for the product on various digital platforms, including social media, at the appropriate time, it will increase the product's visibility among people. Entrepreneurs may advertise in expensive media like digital marketing, social media, hoardings, internet web site, SMS on mobiles, email stalls at exhibitions and fairs, etc. If the entrepreneurs have a comfortable budget, they can resort to advertisements on radio, TV, and in News Papers and Magazines to boost sales by reaching the maximum number of people.

To sum up, entrepreneurs need to understand that the enterprise's success will ultimately come from the sale of the product; therefore, marketing and the sale of the products deserve the highest priority.

•••

CHAPTER 26

# Accounts and Book- Keeping

Accounts and bookkeeping deals with regular and systematic recording of financial transactions professionally as per accounting standards. The accounting of transactions should be done preferably on an advanced version of accounting software like tally prime. The records will enable the entrepreneur to:

a) Keep track record of every transaction.

b) Reflect the corresponding effect of each transaction in other accounting head.

c) It Measure the impact on income, expenses and overall financial position of enterprise and entrepreneurs.

## 1. Need of maintenance of accounts:

It is said that the entrepreneurs who are setting up any type of industry or business enterprise should invariably ensure maintenance of books of accounts from the date of start of the business. If any entrepreneur is not able to build an accounting system, he/she should not start the business. The inefficient system of maintenance of books of accounts may result in the failure of newly set up business enterprises.

Accounts depicts the financial health of business at a given date.

## What is the Bookkeeping:

Booking is the system of recording business transactions in the books of accounts on a regular basis and systematic manner.

## What is Accountancy:

Accounting is the system and procedure of recording, classifying, and summarizing financial transactions.

## How Book-Keeping and Accountancy differs with each other:

Book- Keeping is a primary level of accounting. It only 'record the transactions takes place' where as 'Accountancy' is having a broad spectrum which includes recording, summarizing, analysing and interpreting the financial transactions recorded.

The proper maintenance of the accounts will serve the following purposes:

1) It gives profit or loss position of the business.
2) It gives the current information of outstanding creditors to whom payment is to be made and outstanding debtors from whom the debt is to be recovered.
3) It enables the entrepreneur to undertake comparative study of income and expenditure of current year and previous year, so that he can take the corrective steps to curtail the expenses and increase the income.
4) It helps to know the financial health of the business enterprise to enable the entrepreneur to make the business plan accordingly.
5) It helps to comply with statutory requirements and submission of statutory returns and timely deposit of applicable taxes in the designated accounts of the concerned authorities.
6) It helps to calculate the cost of products and the internal rate of returns from the business
7) It helps in the preparation of investment planning for investing surplus funds.

**Must do to derive maximum benefits from accounts:**

a) Trained and well-experienced person should be appointed for the accountant role.

c) Double entry system with a maker and checker system should be followed.

d) Advance software systems should be used like tally prime.

e) Regular posting of transactions should be done every day.

f] Generate the reports daily to monitor the business of the company.

**Important action points:**

1] Generate a balance sheet and Profit and Loss Account every month and study the strengths and weaknesses of the enterprises.

2] Get the cash flow statement prepared for the next year and compare it with actual figures at monthly intervals.

3] Regularly reconcile the bank statement.

4] cash balance should be tallied regularly

5] Any amount payable should be paid before the due date.

6] Item of expenses should be checked.

7] Entries for refunds and returns should be checked invariably.

8] Debit entries to the profit and loss account should be passed with the permission of the entrepreneur or other competent authority of the enterprise.

9] Timely arrangement of funds should be made if there is a requirement of funds is there in the unit.

10] Surplus funds, if any, should be parked in the bank account in such a way that it earns some interest.

11] Daily vouchers should contain all the details about the transaction and every money should be tallied at the end of the day.

**Types of books and to be maintained.**

1. Cash Book and Bank book.
2. Ledger.
3. Trial balance.
4. General ledger.
5. Contra entries register.
6. Payment register.
7. Receipt register.
8. Debit note/credit note register.
9. Bank reconciliation book.
10. sales register.
11. purchase Register.
12. Stock Register.
13. Dead Stock Register.
14. Salary register.

To sum up, entrepreneurs should introduce an advanced system of accounts and bookkeeping to monitor all the financial transactions in their enterprises and closely supervise and monitor the same to ensure the correctness of transactions and better management of funds available with their enterprises.

•••

CHAPTER 27

# Human Resource Management

Entrepreneurs alone cannot manage their enterprises and will need a mentor and team of people having experience and expertise in the job that will assign to them.

In the beginning stage of a small enterprise, approximately 6 to 7 employees may be sufficient. Entrepreneurs must be careful in recruiting the right person for the right job. A person from finance and accountancy will be suitable for finance and accountancy jobs for enterprises.

Entrepreneurs should select competent people to perform their job with dedication and sincerity. They should be loyal to you and your enterprise and believe in teamwork. While recruiting people apart from their educational background and job-related experience, some psychological assessment is also necessary to have some idea about the positive mindset of the person to become a team member of entrepreneurs.

## 1]. Common Recruitment Sources:

There are multiple sources of recruitment but most commonly sources used by the company for recruitment are as under -

1] Online recruitment portals

2] Referrals from the employees or professional friends

3] Persons working in nearby factories wish to change their job.

4] Universities, institutes, and colleges

5] Social media.

## 1. Recruit the right people for right kind of job:

Entrepreneurs should have a very careful approach in recruitment of people for their enterprises. They should first work out what are job vacancy to be filled immediately or in a phased manner. After that they should specify that what should be the eligibility criteria keeping in view the requirement of the job for the candidates such as –

1] Educational qualification.

2] Experience and expertise.

3] skill

4] Age

The entrepreneurs should also specify what will be the salary and other benefits for each job because the salary and benefits are important considerations for the candidate to accept the job offer. This is also true that highly talented candidates expect higher salary and benefits, but the attrition rate is also high among the highly talented candidates. It's therefore advisable to recruit the average rank candidates so that they can stay with your enterprise for a longer period. Recruitment is a critical issue and therefore entrepreneurs should act as smart professionals and recruit the right kind of person according to the right kind of job for him and remember that the person who has been recruited by you should be able to start the work immediately on his joining. It will be always good to be on lookout for right kind of people so whenever the vacancy arises, you can recruit the people of your choice and you can feel comfortable with their capabilities to handle the job efficiently.

## 3] Recruitment process:

Whatever the sources of recruitment, the structured recruitment process should be followed. First the application in the structured form should be called by the candidates. Thereafter all the applications received should be scrutinized and suitable candidates should be shortlisted for the interview. The interview date and mode of the interview such as on telephone, video call, or in person should be decided and communicated to the candidate. The interview should be conducted systematically by the interviewer to identify whether a person has the skills and abilities for the required job. Once the candidates selected a list of all successful candidates should be prepared, and further process should start for onboarding the selected candidates in a systematic manner.

First, issue a written order to the selected candidates for employment, mentioning therein all the terms and conditions of the appointment. The probation period, if any, should be mentioned invariably in the offer letter. After acceptance of the offer letter by the candidates, a regular appointment letter should be issued and got it accepted by the candidate. After this process the candidate will join on the joining date for that entrepreneurs should obtain the joining letter from the candidate.

## 4. Staff Training programs:

The entrepreneur should consider imparting training to the staff to enable them to perform their job properly. Training for specific skills, if necessary, should also be arranged. It is well known fact that training in the related field to upscale the skills and knowledge will result in better performance of the employees.

## 5] Facilities to employees:

Retention of talented employees is a challenge for the enterprises. Many factors play role in employee's attrition from enterprise. However, the facilities provided to the employees play some role in employees retention. Some of the facilities which can be given to employees must be considered by the employer are as under.

1] Leave entitlement 2] Health insurance 3] Travelling in upper class and lodging and boarding in good hotel while on official duty 4] Success related incentives and appreciation etc. 5] Bonus as per provision of law. 6] contribution to employees' provident fund etc. 7] Regular salary hike based on performance appraisal of the employees, 8] Regular promotion of deserving employees to the higher cadre. All the above facilities will keep the employees moving on their toes for the growth of the enterprise.

To sum up, entrepreneurs should consider the performance link salary and incentive to attract the talented candidate to their team and to overcome the challenges of attrition of employees.

•••

CHAPTER 28

# Time Management

Entrepreneurs need to balance their busy work schedules and personal life, otherwise, it can lead to avoidable work pressure and adversely affect the way we think and make decisions. Hasty decisions can lead to costly consequences. The secret to good corporate governance is good time management. For your business to work like clockwork, you need to manage your time schedule. Poor time management only affects the morale and efficiency of the company's employees. The company's decision-making powers are mostly vested at the managerial level, therefore time management at the managerial level is a must to ensure prompt decisions. Delays in making decisions or responding to problems due to non-availability of the managerial-level executives can be costly business mistakes. Therefore, entrepreneurs must learn, practice, master, and make time management as a part of their life to become successful entrepreneurs.

Once you develop time management skills at work, you will automatically find that you can apply them to other areas of your life.

1. Tools for good time management:
2. Planning of work
3. Prioritization of work
4. Preparation of attending the work

5. Delegate the work to competent employees as per their capabilities.
6. Resource allocation to complete the as planned.
7. Follow up by review of progress of the work.

These tools are guides to good time management practices for both individuals and organizations.

## Time Management Skills:

### Planning of work-

Good planning of the work is the most important aspects of good time management. Knowing what status is as of now and what shall be the future status will help you plan your time more efficiently.

Find out what's going on in your organization. Anything that can impact resources or become a serious problem for the business should be analysed first and resolved as a priority. Prepare the estimation of the bill of quantity and type of work required to address the issue, who will do what, and how long it will take. If Everything you do early in your preparation, it will take your pressure off and can attend other important matters comfortably.

For example, if your company is currently bidding on an important contract for supply of products manufactured by your company. You need to analyse the resources that would be required if the contract were won. You must answer to yourself the question like –

Do you need additional staff? Do your employees need special training to meet the products requirement as per specification given by customers? do you need to change your system? Do you need special equipment? Who will lead the process? What are the key points? What will be the milestones? Knowing the answers of above questions and keeping yourself well prepared, will help you to plan and ensure that your business is ready when the time comes. It not only reduces purchasing pressure, but also ensures customer satisfaction.

Estimating how long a task will take is very important. If accurate estimates are difficult, divide the task into smaller chunks before estimating the entire task at once. Knowing who does what, and in what order is also important. Set deadlines for each milestone and make sure everyone is aware of them.

Preparation and planning are essential for any job, no matter how small.

Get things done properly and on time. Nothing is worse than putting something off until the last minute and then discovering it's taking longer than expected, and having the deadline pushed forward.

Keep a diary and write accurately. Set deadlines for each task or job and make sure you stick to them. Write down everything you need to do each day in a diary and instantly predict how busy you will be the day before.

Check your diary at the end of each day to see if you missed anything!

Once a one chunk of task completed, move it to a new day for next chunk of task and assign a new deadline. Please try to stick to the plan. Unexpected things can happen, but with proper planning, you can minimize the impact on your time.

**Prioritization –**

Evaluate your tasks for the day and come up with a priority system. Critical Tasks, Important Tasks, Mandatory Tasks, and Miscellaneous Tasks. Assign a priority to each task on the list and assign importance within each priority. Once you have that, you can start working on each task in order of importance. Even if the day ends in chaos, at least the important tasks are completed.

Most busy people will tell you that it is amazing how much time you can spend in a day on your work and take out some time to relax also.

If you can get a few things done at once, you can make the most use of every minute.

Instead of waiting to get to the office to check your appointments for the day, do it on your way to the office and save time!

**Preparation –**

If you are prepared, you will not waste your precious time to line up the work. There are many ways to get prepared such as daily status update reports, ongoing work and works holds for you for your approval, and anticipating what you will need at your will can ensure that you are well prepared.

As I said earlier, knowing what is to be done in the future will helps you to allocate resources and make you sure that everything is ready when the time comes. You can add information and keep your notes up to date throughout the month. When a meeting arrives, it's ready in minutes, not hours. It takes less pressure and makes sure you haven't forgotten anything or forgotten anything important.

**Resource Delegation and Allocation –**

Learning to delegate effectively will make you more efficient in comparison to everything you do by yourself. It's about using resources wisely. It doesn't make sense for you to waste 3 hours trying to do something when someone else can do it in his 30 minutes. We tend to waste time looking for information or analysing something when someone else might already have that information. You need to know your employees well, who does what, and what their strengths are. Make the most of your employees' knowledge and skills.

Consider external resources if you need to do something of special nature, as the services of specialists is available in almost every field. Perhaps they have the knowledge, equipment and even better, understanding of the work to be done. This will allow you to handle other, more important issues.

**Follow up –**

Keep track of open issues so you don't panic at the last minute. Making sure that things are going according to plan and that work is progressing steadily will help you feel comfortable as you are sure of meeting deadlines. Procrastinating things until the last minute or noticing that something hasn't been done after the deadline is not good time management.

Distribute and track tasks over time to make sure everything is done and completed on schedule. If something is delayed, find out why. The reason could be that the task was assigned to the wrong person or something unexpected happened.

Keep track of all your tasks and deadlines so you can address issues as they arise while they still have time.

There are many tools and management information systems [MIS], regular monitoring reports, and software applications are there to help you with proper time management. Make the best of every tool available to you and ensure your time management professionally in the best interest of your enterprise and yourself.

●●●

CHAPTER 29

# Crisis Management

Crisis management is a business action plan that is quickly executed when a negative situation arises. Crises disrupt the way an organization does business. Typically, the crises can have negative financial, legal, political, or regulatory consequences, especially if not managed quickly and effectively.

In recent years, we get the news that company has recalled the product particularly from vehicle segment because of some defects noticed after the vehicle is launched in the market, which is classic example of crisis management. In fact, a growing percentage of companies are stepping up efforts to implement effective crisis management strategies as they witness the damage poor crisis management can do to their business enterprise.

Every business has hundreds of potential reasons which create the crises like fires, loss of competitive secrecy, workman strike, defective product, industrial accidents, natural disasters, and system failure, data hacking and many more. A crisis situation may cause financial and reputation loss to a company if not handled properly.

The company should have a crises management plan [CMP] or disaster recovery plan [DRP] and business continuity plan [BCP] so that whenever any crises situation arises, the company comes in action as per their CMP/ DRP and BCP is already in place. It is highly recommended that everyone in the company should be aware of the crises management strategies of the company except in the situation where the crises management is to be handled at the management level only.

It is in the interest of the enterprise to assess whether their industry is sensitive to various crises. They should study the industry data, or work with consultants or subject experts to understand how one or more crises could impact them. Once this process of risk assessment is completed, the enterprise should design a Crisis Management Plan (CMP) to determine how negative events or disaster can be handled effectively to avoid or reduced the loss, even the chances of such of any disaster seems very less. Enterprises should also secure themselves by comprehensive insurance policy, which is the best way to mitigate the risks particularly when such risk or crises arise due to the factors beyond the control of entrepreneurs.

## Sudden crisis:

Many times, the crises are arising suddenly and without any warning such as occupational accidents, natural disasters, sudden death or disability of key management persons, sudden breakdown of IT system, riots and violence etc. and to handle such situation the enterprise should constitute a crises management team, who will take the immediate appropriate action whenever such situation arises.

## Smouldering crisis:

When the enterprise anticipates or has advance notice such as workers strikes, or power cut or there is chain of events which leads to crisis, comes in this category. This type of crisis is to be handled carefully when the entrepreneur notices its first sign and takes the immediate action to mitigate the risk of crises. Sometime these types of crises are difficult to notice but management and employees both should give attention even to smallest signal and should resolve the issues or problems immediately once for all so that such crises do not recur in future.

## Crisis response:

In the event of a crisis, prompt and proactive communication should be the focus of an organization's crisis mitigation strategy. In the crisis, effective communication is critical to positive public perception. It can affect the perceptions of individuals and organizations for a long period after the crisis is over.

Below is a list of some action which enterprises should take when faced with crisis situations and undertaking crises management steps.

1. **Be open and honest with both the media and your customers** – An open and honest attitude with both the media and your customers can certainly inspire the customers and earn the constomer's sympathy, especially when a crisis is largely out of control of the enterprises.

2. **Convey and respond quickly** – Crises situation if it is going to affect the customer's interest adversely, the same should be conveyed to them promptly and correctly and whatever query received from them the same should be responded correctly and quickly.

3. **Use Only One Spokesperson** – There should be one spokesperson who is having the knowledge of the crises should speak with the media if required and to the customers otherwise many persons if they explain the situation, they will do that in their own way, and it may create the confusion among the people and customers.

To sum up, we impress upon the entrepreneurs to make a Crises Management plan or a Disaster management plan together with a Business continuity plan to effectively manage the crises if any such situations arise in their enterprises and maintain business continuity as usual.

•••

CHAPTER 30

# Customer Relationship Management

Customer Relationship Management (CRM) creates a holistic view of customer needs, expectations, and behaviour by analysing information from each customer transaction. CRM creates the customer intelligence on which you need to build customer relationships.

Customer relationship management (CRM) involves the process by which companies track and organize their contacts with current and potential customers. CRM software is used to support these processes; information about customers and customer interactions can be entered, stored, and accessed by employees in different company departments. Typical CRM goals are to improve services provided to customers, and to use customer contact information for targeted marketing.

The term CRM refers to a software-based methods to handle customer relationships, most CRM software vendors recommend a holistic approach. The Success of CRM initiatives depend on understanding of employees to learn and take full advantage of the information systems.

## Overview of CRM:

The customers believe that the business enterprise is a single entity, even though they often interact with many employees of all levels having different roles and responsibilities. CRM is a compact package of policies, processes, and rules being followed by the enterprise to unify its customer interactions and provide ways and means to track customer information. It involves the use of technology in attracting new customers, while retaining existing ones. CRM includes many aspects that are directly related to each other.

i. **Front Office Operations** - This is the process of direct interaction with customers by way of face-to-face, telephone, email, online services, etc.

ii. **Back-office operations** - Back-office operations ultimately affect front office activities (e.g., billing, maintenance, scheduling of work relating to customer service, marketing, advertising, finance, manufacturing, etc.)

iii. **Business Relationships** — These covers interactions with other companies and business partners, suppliers, Dealers and Retailers, industry Networks (Lobby, Groups, Trade Associations) etc. This external network supports front office and back-office activities.

iv. **Analytics** - Analyses key CRM data to plan targeted marketing, designing campaigns, strategies to increase the sales, and evaluating the success of CRM measures (e.g., market share, number and type of customers, sales volume, profitability).

## Types and variations of CRM:

There are different CRM approaches with different software packages that focus on different aspects. In general, customer service, campaign management, and sales automation form the core of the system.

i. **Operational CRM** - Operational CRM supports business processes relating to sales force automation, managing sales campaigns, Marketing, post sales services etc. Customer interactions are typically stored in the customer's contact history, allowing the concerned employee to retrieve customer information as needed.

ii. **Sales Intelligence CRM** - Sales Intelligence CRM is having features like sending alerts to sales staff for new selling opportunities, customer trends, cross selling of products, etc.

Customer drift Sales performance, Customer trends, Customer margins, Customer alignment, and Collaborative CRM, covers aspects of a company's dealings with customers that are handled by various departments within a company, such as sales, technical support and marketing. Employees from different departments can share information gleaned from customer interactions. For example, feedback received from an accountant, his/her manager may provide other employees with information about services or features requested by customers. The ultimate goal of collaborative CRM is to use the information collected from all departments to improve the quality of service provided by the company.

iii. **Consumer Relations system** - Consumer Relations System "CRS" Covers aspects of consumer affairs within the organization handled by the Customer Relations Contact Centre. It provides early warning of product issues (such as item recalls) and track consumer's sentiments.

iv. **Geographic CRM** - Geographic CRM (GCRM) is a combination of Geographic Information System and traditional CRM. Geographic data can be analysed to provide a snapshot of prospects within a region or to plan routes for customer visits.

## Strategy:

Several CRM software packages are available with different

approaches to CRM. However, as mentioned earlier, CRM is more than just technology, it is a holistic, customer-centric approach to an organization's customer-facing philosophy. This includes policies and processes, front office customer service, employee training, marketing, systems, and information management. Therefore, it's important that CRM implementation extends beyond technology to the wider needs of the organization. The goals of your CRM strategy are to consider your customers' needs and expectations, as well as your company's specific policy. Information collected through CRM initiatives helps organizations in areas such as onboarding new customer segments, improving existing customer retention, improving product offerings through a better understanding of customer needs, and identifying the organization's high value customers and providing appropriate knowledge for the development of marketing strategies.

CRM strategies vary in size, complexity, and scope. CRM strategies should cover customer interactions across the enterprises with sales, marketing, event management, project management, and financial functionality.

## Data protection and data safety:

One of the main functions of CRM software is to collect information about customers. When collecting data as part of a CRM solution, companies should consider their customer's desires for privacy and data security, as well as legal and cultural norms. Some customers prefer to double-check that data is not shared with third parties without prior consent and that safeguards are in place to prevent unlawful access by third parties.

To sum up, entrepreneurs should make the best possible use of the CRM system to ensure customer satisfaction, increase repeat sales, and onboard new customers to increase sales and scale up their business enterprises.

●●●

CHAPTER 31

# Failure of Enterprises – Symptoms, Reasons and Remedy

We all are aware that after some period from the date of establishment of the unit, some units start showing signs of sickness. Before any unit becomes sick it gives an early warning signal and entrepreneurs should keep a close watch on these early warning signals. They should identify the problem, and its reasons and take the appropriate action at the early stage before the small problem turns into a big problem. The unit is treated as a sick unit if it has made a loss in the previous year and going to make a loss in the current financial year also. We discuss hereunder in detail, the warning signal/symptoms, reasons/causes, and remedy to prevent the sickness or failure of enterprises.

## 1. Warning signals of the unit going towards sickness are as mentioned below:

a) Capacity utilization reduced.

b) Liquidity crunch and therefore not in a position to meet financial liabilities on time.

c) Non submission/delayed submission of stock statement and other monitoring statements to banks.

d) Increase in sundry creditors due to non-payment of their dues in time.

e) Mis management of inventory as supplier do not supply the material on credit.

f) Unsatisfactory conduct of bank account. Delay in payment of term loan instalments.

g) Frequent request to banks for Temporary overdraft.

h) Decline in sales turnover and profit.

i) Delay in payment of taxes.

j) Timely auditing of books of accounts not done.

k) High attrition rate of employee.

**2. The causes/reasons of failure of business enterprises may be one or more and can be divided in to two categories with remedial measure as below:**

**i. External factors responsible for failure of unit:**

a) Change in the government policy, particular products are banned by the government. -

Reasons - Govt policy may change as per the socio-economic development plan, harmful impact on the environment due to products or processes, or any other reasons.

Remedy - Change or modify the product in accordance with govt policy. Keep informed with the upcoming changes in the Govt policy and take action to modify or change the product or process if possible or change the business activity itself in case no other options are available.

b) Natural calamities - Drought, flood, Pandemic and Fire etc.-

Remedy - Every enterprise should have a Disaster management team and team should start the action immediately to minimize the loss and help the business to continue.

c) Other external factors – Fire, theft, burglaries, strike, system breakdown, market recessionary trend etc.

Remedy – [For b and c]. Enterprises should have a Disaster management team and team should start the action immediately to minimize the loss and help the business continuity team to continue the business of the enterprises. Comprehensive Insurance policy must be obtained covering eligible risk to the maximum extent to protect the unit from the loss if such situation mentioned in point no. a] and b] above arises.

### ii. Internal factors responsible for failure of unit:

These factors are directly related to the weakness in the working of the unit. Reason lies in the entrepreneurs or in the enterprises in any one or all its functionalities. We discuss hereunder the internal factors responsible for failure of unit and the remedies available to prevent the failure of the unit.

a) Entrepreneurs always require to be a thought leader and build a team of competent personnels. They should cultivate the culture of team spirit in their enterprises. Entrepreneurs should believe in proper delegation of powers to their team members. Wherever the entrepreneurs or their key management personnel do not take the right decision at the right time, the enterprises cannot perform well. Teamwork is necessary for the success of the enterprises.

Remedy – The entrepreneurs are expected to develop leadership qualities so that they can run their enterprises successfully.

b) Selection of wrong products – If products are not selected or updated/improved from time to time after proper market study of demand and supply position, customer's need, choice, preference or market trend, the product may not pick up sale volume or sale volume start declining.

Remedy - Entrepreneurs should make changes in their products as per market demand from time to time keeping in view the customer's needs and choices. Even printing and packaging should also be developed as per preference of the customers and market trend.

c) Selection of old technology-based plant and machinery- The old technology-based plant and machinery will have less capacity, more wastage, poor quality products with a high cost of production. This all makes the products less finished, and entrepreneur must price it more under compulsion keeping in consideration of high cost of production which have combining effect of declining in market share in comparison to other competitors having latest technology-based machines and because of that their cost of production comes less and therefore they can price their products on lower side.

   Remedy - The entrepreneur should always go for latest technology-based plant and machinery.

d) Delay in implementation of project and achieving commercial operation date - This kind of delay in completion of project and achieving commercial operation date shall increase the cost of project and will have adverse effect on project profitability.

   Remedy - Entrepreneurs should follow the implementation strictly and start commercial operation on the date fixed for that purpose.

e) Delay in sanction and disbursement of loan - This may delay the project if term loan is delayed and it will delay the production of goods if the working capital is not sanctioned or released in time, which are not desirable for achieving targeted production and sales volume of the enterprises as per their business plan.

Remedy - The entrepreneurs should submit their credit proposals well in advance and answer all the queries if any asked by the banks as fast as possible so that the credit facility can be sanctioned and disbursed by the bank on time.

f) Power shortage - This may hamper production if there is a power shortage or frequent power cut in the factory area.

   Remedy - Entrepreneurs should have the provision of a power generator to overcome the power shortage/power cut, so that their production process is not hampered.

g) Non availability of skilled/unskilled labour - This aspect directly affects production if the labours of desired skilled or unskilled labours are not available.

   Remedy - The enterprises should have proper human resource management policy and benefits as prevalent industry trend with some extra benefits. This will motivate the workers to work in your enterprises.

h) Fund diversion - If working capital funds are diverted for the creation of fixed assets or non-current assets it will create a shortage of working capital funds and unit may find it difficult to purchase the raw material and meet operational expenses. This will lead to a decline in production and ultimately sales. Apart from the above funds are siphoned out from the unit for some other use, which will also create a working capital shortage for the unit. Fund diversion or siphoning out of the funds is treated with disfavour by the bank and the bank shall recall all the credit facilities from the borrowers.

   Remedy - Entrepreneurs should never divert the funds internally or siphon out the funds for some other use outside the enterprises even for temporary purposes.

i) Operational or technical problem - Many times operational problems arise in the day to day running of the unit or there may be sudden breakdown of machinery or system which may lead to decline in production.

   Remedy - Unit should have proper personnel to handle the problem and restore the production as soon as possible.

j) Absence of proper Marketing strategies- The marketing of the product is main aspect of business enterprises which bring the sales, but if proper marketing strategies or market study and status of demand and supply is not in place, it may affect the sales of the unit drastically. Likewise, the study of market competition from other competitors is also important to make the proper market strategies.

   Remedy - The entrepreneurs should update their marketing strategies from time to time, continue to conduct market study, analyse the data of demand and supply position, customer's needs and take feedback of customers. The entrepreneurs should collect information on quality and prices of the products from competitors and their market share and accordingly they should make their marketing strategies to win the better share of their product in the market.

To sum up, entrepreneurs should keep a close watch on the warning signals of sickness, and on observing any signal relating to sickness in the enterprises, they should take remedial measures immediately.

•••

CHAPTER 32

# Leadership

Leadership is one of the important aspects which must be developed by every human being. Effective leadership is required to lead and guide the subordinates to perform organizational tasks effectively and efficiently. Leadership is the activity of influencing people to strike willingly for group objectives. It's worth quoting the following thoughts here-

"True leadership lies in guiding success -in ensuring that everyone is performing all their best, doing they are pledged to do and doing it well" – Bill ovens [Graciousquotes.com]

"Leadership is not a position or title; it is action and example" - Cory Booker [ www.Idleheart.com]

The above quotes are self-explanatory and convey what leadership means. We discuss here under the following aspect of leadership:

## A] Characteristics of successful leaders. -

1] **Health conscious** – It is a famous quote that "health is wealth. The leaders know importance of physical and mental fitness to work with full potential, remain active and alert, feel energetic to achieve their goal. Entrepreneurs should always keep themselves physically and mentally healthy.

2] **Communication-** The communication is an art and science of conveying message written or verbal completely without any distortion from one person to another person or group. The leaders always effectively convey their messages maintaining clarity of expression, well organised, politeness and courtesy in their messages so that the person or people should receive the message in same meaning and same sense in which the messages are sent. Entrepreneurs should learn the skill and style of effective communication.

3] **Cool and calm** - The leaders keep themselves cool and calm in every situation thick or thin because they know that they can take the right decision when they remain cool and calm state of mind. Entrepreneurs should also keep themselves cool and calm and maintain their balance of mind to take the right decision at the right time irrespective of situation.

4] **Delegation-** Leaders believe in delegation of powers to the down the line executives so that their executives take the decision on time and need not to wait for decision from the leaders. This will expedite the decision-making process and works are completed in a faster way. The Entrepreneurs should also make it a practice to delegate the powers down the line and guide their executive to take the decision with courage and confidence even if any of the decision go wrong, the leaders protect the executives if they have taken the decisions in good faith and in the interest of the organization. The entrepreneurs may involve in some other important work if they believe in capabilities of their executive and delegate the powers because if they try to attend everything it's going to be a tough task for them.

5] **Not argue but discuss-** Leaders do not make argument to through their ideas to implement but they discuss their ideas with their team, listen the views of the team, get convince or make them convinced by healthy discussions and then take the appropriate decision to implement the ideas.

This practice makes every team member to feel happy that their viewpoints are always taken into consideration by their leader. Entrepreneurs should also adopt the same approach of participation of their team in decision making process with practicing of healthy discussions.

6] **Knowledge and skill** – Successful leaders always invest in themselves to enhance their knowledge and skills and learn and adopt the latest processes and techniques related to their work and keep them updated on latest developments in all other areas at national as well as international. Entrepreneurs should also invest in themselves to enhance their knowledge and skills for their successful entrepreneurial journey.

7] **Focused Approach and team spirit** – Leaders believe in team spirit and have their focused approach to achieve their goal as per their vision and mission with the support of their team. They do not divert their attention on other things easily and keep on moving ahead as per their strategic plan to achieve their goal with the support of their team. Entrepreneurs should also have the above approach to achieve their goal.

8] **Thought leader** - The successful leaders are thought leaders who inspire the others with their knowledge, experience, and expertise in their work as well as their awareness about what is happening all around. The thought leaders are having very positive outlook towards life and built in character of great human being.

## It is relevant to quote here-

If your actions inspire others to dream more, learn more, do more, and become more, you are a leader. - John Quincy Adams [www.businessmanagementblog.com]

The entrepreneurs should be the thought leaders and inspire others by virtue of establishing their authority as an expert in a specific area of their working, building a trust among employees and customers and providing innovative solutions to industry challenges and innovative products, process, and services to the world. This will make their enterprise outstanding among the other enterprises, and they become the source of inspiration to others in addition to winning performance of their own enterprise.

## B] Roles and responsibilities of leaders. -

Leaders are having various role/responsibilities of which are discussed here under:

1. **Goal fixation:**

   The leadership must set the goals and objectives for their enterprises and sensitize their entire team to achieve the goal. Goal setting is one of the important functions of the leaders. The goals may be set up by the leaders themselves, or they may take the help of their management team in goal setting.

2. **Develop high Morale of their employee:**

   One of the important functions of a leaders is to develop high morale in their employees. They always strive hard to keep their employees happy, so that they can enjoy their work. They always try to develop a positive attitude of their employees.

3. **Participation in growth:**

   The leaders influence the employees to work willingly towards achievements of objectives of the enterprises. Good leaders always motivate the employees to work hard and smart, and as a team member with other employees. Leaders takes an active part in the activities of the team as a team member.

4. **Initiative and suggestions:**

   Leaders welcome new innovative suggestions and ideas from the employees for the growth of the enterprises. They create a healthy environment in which employees work as a team to fulfil the objectives of the enterprises.

5. **Team Spirit:**

   The leaders give priority in team building in their enterprises. In case if any difference of opinion arises among their employees, they strive hard to resolve the differences so that team spirit is maintained in the interest of enterprise. Good leaders believe in "WE" and not "I" policy.

6. **Opportunity:**

   The leaders provide the opportunity to their employees to participate in various forums, meetings, and conferences to express their views with higher authorities within or outside of the enterprises.

7. **Building confidence:**

   Good leaders build confidence in their employees. They make them courageous to take decisions in the interest of enterprises even in adverse situations and to teach them how to face the challenges keeping the balance of mind in challenging situations.

8. **Friend, philosopher, and guide:**

**It is worth to quote here-**

"A good objective of leadership is to help those who are doing poorly to do well and to help those who are doing well to do even better" – Jim Rohn [success.com]

Effective leaders work with the team as a friend, philosopher, and guide, improve their skills, and competencies to their full potential and keep the team highly motivated to work for the organization dedicatedly, and diligently to achieve the organizational goal.

To sum up, we want to impress upon entrepreneurs to become leaders, reach the level of thought leaders, and effectively lead their teams to achieve their goals.

**XXX**

# Acknowledgement

First, I would like to thank the Almighty for giving me this wonderful life, and inspiring, loving, and caring parents, my father late, Shri Babulal Jain, and my mother, the late Smt. Shanta bai Jain. I always feel their presence with me, which gives me the strength to face life's challenges and keeps me moving.

Secondly, a big thanks to my wife, Smt. Sunita Jain for being with me in all thick and thin positions and supporting me to keep working, not for my own or family but for society in general and the young entrepreneurs in particular.

Thirdly I express big thanks to my son Abhishek who is always taking our best care in all possible ways. He always inspires me to share my expertise and experience with the people at large and help them start their entrepreneurial journey: Abhishek, my big hug to you for being a lovely son.

I also express my special thanks to Shri Amit Goel, Managing Director of Prodigee Finance Ltd, who constantly inspires me to write this book to benefit youth looking for self-employment opportunities to become successful startup entrepreneurs.

Last but not least, I thank you very much to all the readers who picked up this book to become unstoppable startup entrepreneurs. I am grateful to all of you for your encouragement to continue my mission to spread and support entrepreneurship development worldwide. Please keep this book always with you, not only as a book but as your friend, philosopher, and guide in your entrepreneurial journey. Please give feedback/reviews about this book on the platform from where you purchased it so that other aspirant entrepreneurs will be encouraged to read it to start their entrepreneurial journey.

Thanking you all.

With profound regards.

**Dr. Suresh Jain**

**[Author]**